JEAN-CLAUDE GAUTRAND

PHOTOGRAPHERS' PARIS

Dorset Press
New York

50660

Paris: city of light. During the Twenties, Hemingway called Paris "a moveable feast," a wonderful, endless party that stimulated the intellect and intoxicated the senses. "The last time I saw Paris," goes the song by Oscar Hammerstein II, "her heart was warm and gay, / I heard the laughter of her heart in every street cafe." Utrillo and Caillebotte painted her streets, Renoir and Toulouse-Lautrec her cabarets. Blaise Cendrars wrote: "I could spend my whole life / Watching the Seine flow by . . / It is a poem of Paris."

Novelists, songwriters, painters and poets have long sought to capture the essence of this beguiling city. But perhaps no group of artists has succeeded as well as the great photographers of the nineteenth and twentieth centuries. *Photographers' Paris* pays tribute to their artistry.

Paris has been a favorite subject of photographers since Daguerre invented his daguerréotype there more than 150 years ago. *Photographers' Paris* introduces you to the work of those great early photographers: To Daguerre's formal images of the Parisian skyline with their remote and evanescent beauty; to Charles Nègre's dramatic street scenes and character studies; to Charles Marville's haunting alleys and his compelling chronicles of Baron Haussmann's wholesale renovations of the city at mid-century; to Eugène Atget's photographic elegies to the vanishing street vendors of fin-de-siècle Paris.

Photographers' Paris offers a visual feast of every aspect of the city—of both the old Paris and its modern counterpart. Here are captivating images of the Boulevards, the Seine, Montmartre and Les Halles taken by the great names in photography: Cartier-Bresson, Alfred Stieglitz, Robert Doisneau, Willy Ronis, André Kertész, Man Ray and many others. If you have ever wondered why Paris has so often been called the most romantic city on earth, then leaf through the following pages. You will soon understand why.

On July 1, 1822, in the Paris of the Restoration period of King Louis XVIII, people were crowded together at the opening of a new artistic venture, situated in the fashionable neighborhood of the Faubourg du Temple. All of the witnesses to this event were struck with amazement: Immense screens, expertly rendered, depicted spacious landscapes or sumptuous interiors such as Saint-Etienne-du-Mont. The novelty and the particular interest of this spectacle were to be found in the gradual changes of scenes. Thanks to the subtle play of light, scenes blended as they succeeded each other in front of the spectators' eyes.

Enraptured by a church interior lit by the sunlight streaming through the stained glass, with the darkness snaking away through the nave and the choir as the lights came on, the erstwhile spectators became the congregation of the faithful for a veritable mass, celebrated with great pomp and accompanied by the sound of church bells. This highly effective aural and optical illusion, this dexterity in the use of light and sound together with the perfection of these pictures achieved an instant triumph. *The Foreigners' Guide to Paris* emphatically recommended a visit to the Diorama, which had become an instant and stupendous success.

The inventor of this spectacle, who enjoyed such fame that two years later he was admitted to the *Legion d'honneur*, was Louis-Jacques Mandé Daguerre. One Diorama visitor was the inventor Nicéphore Niepce, who was so impressed that he wrote: "I haven't seen anything here (in Paris) that has struck me more, which I enjoyed more than the Diorama.—" Out of Niepce's encounter with the work of Daguerre, photography, and its long romance with Paris, was born.

Daguerre was a man of the world. He enjoyed the company of painters, actors and writers. A theater scene-painter and a tireless worker, he made tremendous use of the camera obscura to capture, on his enormous screens, the fleeting images of his day. The equipment for his innovative work was purchased from Charles Chevalier, the famous optician, who had a shop at the end of the quai de l'Horloge across from the statue of Henri IV. Chevalier's shop was to be the scene of encounters and events presaging the birth of photography. There, in the shadow of the Pont-Neuf, Chevalier sold glasses, optical instruments and cameras to many would-be photographers attempting to imitate life. Daguerre, who dedicated all his spare time to studying the various ways of capturing and fixing the images of the camera obscura, was one of his regular customers.

Nicéphore Niepce had long occupied himself with similar research. In fact, his work was plainly more advanced than Daguerre's; he had already succeeded in fixing on pewter plates reproductions of engravings, and had experimented with "point de vue" in pictures taken from the window of his house at Gras. He too was a customer of Chevalier, who was responsible for introducing the two men. After a period of mutual distrust, they started working together, their collaboration lasting until Niepce's death in 1833. Daguerre continued their research and succeeded in perfecting a method of reproduction using silver plate, which he simply called "daguerréotype." With this silver plate he made photographs first in his studio and soon after, in the streets of the capital. Thus were born the first pictures of Paris. Arago, director of the Observatory, took an interest in this development and advised the government to buy the process and put it on the market. On August 11, 1839, the case was settled, and excited Parisians thronged into the Chamber of Deputies to celebrate the advent of the age of photography.

That very evening Paris was impregnated with the smells of mercury, hyposulfite and silver oxide. The next day the opticians' shops were besieged, the chemists' cleaned out! Armed with their cameras obscura—luxurious ones or crudely constructed ones in cardboard boxes—passionate experimenters photographed furniture or tried to reproduce the view from the window. According to Marc-Antoine Gaudin: "Fortunate was the one who caught the outline of the rooftops with his first shot; he went into ecstasy in front of the stove-pipes; he kept on counting the roof tiles and the row of chimneys. In short, from the most insignificant print he obtained the most unspeakable delight." Several days later, scores of daguerréotypes, fixed onto their tripods, were focused throughout the city on the principal statues. Those cameras, heavy and bulky, well-constructed but prohibitively expensive—about 400 francs, which would take the average worker 200 workdays to accumulate—had become the latest toys of the well-to-do, a diverse group comprising merchants, scientists and painters.

To satisfy public curiosity, Daguerre gave several demonstrations of his photographic plates; these included the pavilion of Flore, the Île de la Cité, pictures of Parisian boulevards, the banks of the Seine, the Pont-Neuf, the famous statues, and panoramic views from the top of Notre-Dame or the Church of Saint-Gervais. Fragile and delicate, these pictures were the first to capture the Paris of 1840. Even though, due to the long exposure time, no human life is to be seen: The city is as turned to stone, enchanted.

In spite of the drawbacks of the process—a single print of a shimmering, fragile quality and with the image often reversed—these early prints are doubly valuable: they bear witness not only to the birth of photography, but also to medieval Paris, the last vestiges of which would disappear in a decade. The Paris of the daguerréotype is still a unique metropolis enlivened by a sparkling intellectual life; a "universal city" where, as Goethe had written a few years before, "each footstep on a bridge, on a square, brings back a great past, where at each street corner a fragment of history unrolls." Yet Paris, complex and ambiguous in its diversity, was also admired by those who, setting aside the grandeurs of history, loved, as did Balzac, this city of "somber landscapes," of "bursts of light," of "deep and quiet culs-de-sac."

I n the 1840s, France was experiencing many changes under the reign of Louis Philippe. The population of Paris was growing all the time and there were now one million inhabitants. The sidewalks became longer and, while the water carriers still made their rounds through town, their pails on their shoulders, the very first gas burners were installed. The Île Louviers was connected to the right bank; the boulevards were fixed up and leveled (today we only have the Boulevards Saint-Martin and Bonne-Nouvelle to give us an idea of their former circular configuration). The statue of the emperor was placed on top of the Vendôme pillar; the Place de la Concorde was renovated, the Obelisque erected in its center; the Arc de Triomphe was unveiled; and the first "departure platforms" (which is what train stations were called at the time) were opened. But in 1839, the literary, artistic and political circles were mainly interested in the birth of the prodigious, new way of reproduction: photography. The astounding precision of the daguerréotypes symbolized the attainment of perfection in the eyes of those nineteenth-century people for whom art above all, had to be an exact representation of nature.

A great many painters, conscious of the many possibilities of this new process, became photographers and opened ateliers and studios. Ingres, speaking for others as well, was troubled by what he called the blend of industry and art, acknowledging privately that photography represented "the kind of precision that I would like to attain. It's beautiful; photography is very beautiful, but it doesn't do to say so." The inherent shortcomings of the process itself (already listed above), inspired several photographers to search for another way of obtaining the darkroom picture. The discussions and arguments about art and the recent discoveries abounded in the salons and ateliers. Armaury Duval, a student of Ingres and an artist and reporter of repute, had one of the most famous salons. Among its habitués were Charlet, a remarkable technician; Grevedon, renowned portrait painter and a friend of Daguerre; the engraver Gavrani; the book illustrator Bertall; the painter Ziegler; and Hyppolyte Bayard, a humble clerk of the ministry of Finance. Bayard, his working day over, intensely enjoyed passionate moments in the middle of this artistic and literary circle, delighting in the eclectic conversation and in the discussion of new ideas. He obviously knew the famous Diorama on the Place du Chateau-d'Eau and was aware of Daguerre's invention. The subject excited him and he in his turn threw himself into the adventure of looking for a new method, producing his efforts on paper instead of metal.

On March 20, 1839, Bayard obtained straight positive pictures. Arago advised him to reveal nothing about his discovery so as not to harm Daguerre's reputation. Bayard was quiet for a month but then on June 24, on the occasion of a benefit for the victims of an earthquake in Martinique, he assembled in large frames, twenty proofs that he presented together with his canvases. This photo exposition, the first in the world, took place in Paris, in the Hall of the Official Appraisers, and had tremendous repercussions in artistic and scientific circles. *Le Moniteur* and *Le Constitutionnel* reported the news. Across the Channel, the Englishman Fox Talbot, working in the same direction, discovered that same year a method by which he was able to obtain negative pictures on paper, which on contact would give positive pictures. With the appearance of positive and negative prints, photography as we know it today saw the light. The era of unlimited reproduction had begun. The process was baptized *calotype* from the Greek *kalos* for beauty.

During the 1850s the French school of photography became famous throughout the world through the names of Baldus, Blanquart-Evrard, Ducamp, Davanne, Marville, Le Gray, Nègre, Regnault, Louis Robert, and Le Secq, among others. It was, truly, the golden age of photography! We can date the beginning of this era from 1847 when Regnault produced a remarkable series of portraits of members of the Académie des Sciences, and Bayard began to daguerréotype several monuments in Paris. The capital was about to become the capital of photography.

Eighteen fifty-one was a banner year for photography. Blanquart-Evrard opened the first photo-printer's workshop and for the next five years it published a great number of works illustrated with photographs glued in by hand. In the Rue de l'Arcade in Paris, the first photographic society in the world was founded, the *Société heliographique*, uniting, at the instigation of the baron of Montfort, numerous personalities such as Bayard and his friend Jules Ziegler, Becquerel, Benjamin Delessert, Niepce de Saint-Victor, Mestral, the count of Aguado, Lerebours and Chevalier (whose importance we have already noted). It was an association that aspired to be "purely artistic and scientific, of men devoted to study and to the application of arts and science." Two years later this society was dissolved and some of its most eminent members founded in 1853 the French Society of Photography, which played an essential role in Paris and became a focal point of encounters for the majority of practicing photographers. The photographic journal *La Lumière* was also founded in Paris in 1851, and a new process, *collodion humide*, which used a solution of powdered cotton, was invented by the Englishman Scott Archer. The process marked the end of calotype and the beginning of the period of the great portraitists who, opening their luxurious salons, became eminent personalities all over Paris.

The infatuation with photography that existed in certain circles was not simply a result of chance. The July Monarchy of 1830 that brought Louis Philippe to the throne benefitted the upper middle class (the bankers and the captains of industry), giving it the support of a regime that was against any innovation, that distanced itself from extremes and that delighted in nationalistic sentiment. The new regime supported the artists of "the right circles," such as Delaroche and Horace Vernt who made large historical frescoes and avoided everything that might clash with conformity: an average art for a ruling class of an average level. But the republican political opposition, which Arago took part in, was particularly receptive to the new ideas and to scientific research. The republicans welcomed photography, which, because of its nature, was automatically linked to the new movement of realism—"by essence the democratic art," as Courbet declared. On a political level conservatives and liberals responded to the artistic struggle of the romantics and realists respectively. Renouncing pure art and affirming its social role, realism emphasized before everything else the direct observation of the subject. Photography, obviously destined for the purpose, was in high favor with this movement. Didn't the photographers and painters of the Barbizon school catch their subjects outside and under the same natural light? The calotype was excellent for this, and the realists found themselves celebrating the naturalistic pictures of the great calotypists—pictures of landscapes, old streets and prestigious monuments.

Among the photographers who would catapult to its zenith the so-called Paris School, many were painters by origin. Le Secq, Joseph Nègre and Fenton frequented the atelier Delaroche, set up in the rear wing of the *Institut de France*. Delaroche was counted among the first supporters of photography and didn't hesitate to recommend its use to his students. Gustave Le Gray, student of père Picot, had a studio near the gates of Clichy. These calotypists, who would be joined by other famous practitioners, made up a nucleus of artists in the minority. The majority of artists remained close to "the right circles", which was easily explained by their relatively comfortable background.

Facing this official conformism, Paris gave birth to a kind of intellectual proletarianism that was to inject new life into art and photography. Minor clerks, craftsmen, students, writers and journalists, among them Champfleur, Murger, Delveau and Nadar, began to meet in several cafés in the Latin quarter. Then there was another group made up of figures from artistic and literary circles—Théofile Gautier, Gérard de Nerval, Camille Rogier and others—who formed a new Bohemia, the "Jeune France." Enlightened, progressive and politically active, this bohemian group participated in the many movements that stirred up Paris in the 1840s. Politically antibourgeois, artistically opposed to the world of money and industry that wanted to mold everything, including the domain of art, to its own standards, the members of Jeune France began to combat the dominant aesthetic ideas.

When the February Revolution broke out in 1848, Nadar was whole-heartedly on the side of the rebels. Bayard photographed the remains of the barricade in the Rue Royale. Charles Nègre joined the national guard and stood guard (appropriately) at the Louvre. Niepce de Saint-Victore, lieutenant of the municipal guard, watched his laboratory, located in the barracks of the district of Saint-Martin, being ransacked by the delirious crowd. Louis Philippe abdicated.

The prince-president, Louis Napoleon Bonaparte, was elected later that year. In December 1852, after a referendum involving 7,800,000 Frenchmen, Napoleon III was installed at the Tuileries. Thus, the Second Empire succeeded the mediocre "right circles" of Louis Philippe and, during the following twenty years, would preside over the great industrial revolution of the nineteenth century.

The insular world of photography, in the bosom of which artists and scientists pursued their research and experiments, was not troubled by this political upset. Scott Archer's discovery of a process based on collodion spurred photographic research. Le Gray established a laboratory on the Rue de Richelieu where he impregnated the paper with raw melted beeswax before covering it with collodion. By this technique Le Gray attained such consistency and transparency that calotype enjoyed renewed popularity. At the Paris World's Fair of 1850 he submitted nine of his photographs produced by this method. Although astonished by their quality, the jury refused after much deliberation to allow them in the exhibition under the pretext that they weren't works of art but products of science!

The calotypists were not discouraged and continued with their work. Charles Nègre moved to Paris from Cannes, and eventually set up shop at 21 Quai de Bourbon on the Île Saint-Louis, where he joined a large community of artists who had taken up residence there: Meissonnier, Daumier, Prévost, Préault and Baudelaire. He found their company especially stimulating, although he continued to attend the meetings organized by the *Société heliographique*. After 1850 Nègre became a familiar figure, lugging his heavy camera obscura down the street, and started photographing Parisian buildings, bridges and monuments. He excelled in architectural photos, as did many calotypists, but he distinguished himself from them in that he was the first to disclose photography's fabulous power to capture life itself. In the yard by his house and everywhere on the Île Saint-Louis, he set out to record numerous street scenes. Although the first of those, such as "The Little Chimney-sweeps," were posed, many were possessed of the drama that distinguished his later snapshots. Indeed, his "Fall of a Horse on the Quai de Bourbon" was perhaps the first news photo.

Nègre's friend Le Secq, who often accompanied him on these photographic walks through Paris, appears in a number of his pictures, in particular the famous photo "The Gargoyle" taken on one of the towers of the Notre-Dame. Nègre continued his strolls through the streets of the capital and photographed many architectural monuments and treasures. Several of these pictures were published by Blanquart-Evrard in his book *Paris photographique 1851*, side by side with works by Charles Marville. These precious pictures, preserved almost in their totality at the *Arts décoratifs* library, testify to a Paris that was quickly changing and would soon undergo the worst difficulties and hardships.

The timid prefect Rambuteau, replaced by Berger in 1852, had already started the first urban works, which were later enormously expanded by Baron Haussmann. Le Secq witnessed these events, photographing the old houses and the first demolition sites.

The first negatives dedicated to Paris by Charles Marville appeared in 1851. With the use of "waxed" negative paper, he could fashion prints of remarkable quality. Onto his evocative backgrounds, often uninhabited by people, he painted in his russet, grainy, dense pictures, creating romantic images of Paris. Like his contemporaries he stuck to photographing topography and architecture. In contrast with Le Secq's precise rendering of detail and beguiling sense of light, Marville emphasized a rigorous analysis of settings and environment. This is the case in the photos representing the removing of the fountain at Châtelet, the church of Saint-Germain-l'Auxerrois, the Pont-Neuf, or that fantastic photo with its Brueghellian atmosphere of the Fountain of the Innocents surrounded by its old market.

Marville's first pictures were brilliant, but the pictures of Paris that followed would equal if not surpass them. A great number of these were published in the books of Blanquart-Evrard. Marville loved, understood and illustrated Paris as well as any photographer. His name ranks with Nègre, Le Secq, Atget, and the great picture-takers of the capital: Maxime du Camp, Eugène Piot, Félix Teynard, Baldus, Salzmann and Bisson, to name a few. Their prints that have survived, though often yellowed, reveal a mastery of technique coupled with a profound affection for Paris and its people.

The 1849 Exposition of Industrial Products was the first official exposition to show photographs (a majority of which were portraits) by Millet, Plumier, the brothers Bisson and Martens. It was a highly influential forum, but it was the World's Fair of 1855—the year considered by Lacan to bridge the primitive age and the modern age—that would significantly affect the course of photography in the late nineteenth century.

The development of industry, the progress of science and the social transformations of the nineteenth century obviously led to changes in the way the world was thought about and represented. The tendency toward objectivity found its philosophical expression in the positivist movement (Taine) and its artistic illustration in the school of realists (Courbet). This new form of truth drew even more attention to photography, which by 1855 was mostly practiced by a certain intellectual elite in Paris. The 1855 World's Fair featured a special section on photography. Although the public, like the jury of the *Exposition des beaux arts* before it, had rejected the work of Courbet and the realists, people now came in droves to admire the true-to-nature copies of these works offered by photographers (most of whom practiced portraiture, then becoming more and more popular in Paris).

But already a different kind of picture was appearing, not only showing street scenes, but also, in the pictures of Nègre and Disdéri, the strolling passers-by. Parisians and provincials, crowding in at the gates of the exposition, were discovering the new possibilities of photography. However, the future could lead each of these photographers in quite different directions, and some were to come into conflict, depending on how each adapted to the commercial market.

Gustave Le Gray, for example, had attained his peak by 1855. He left his atelier in the Rue de Richelieu and moved into a large brick house located on the corner of the Boulevard de Capucines and the Rue Saint-Augustin. The quarter of the Madeleine, a bit inconveniently situated at that time on the outskirts of Paris, was not yet very popular. This same large building housed two other photographers, the Bisson brothers, who were financed by the Dolfusses from Mulhouse, on the ground floor, and another photographer, De Marnhya, who opened a studio for photo-sculpture on the first floor. It was an astonishing concentration of talent. The Bisson's store soon became all the rage, in part because Paris had started expanding westward. The two brothers exhibited large, splendid prints of mountain landscapes. Attracted by the luxury of the store and the perfection of the pictures, browsers would come in and meet the more illustrious visitors, who were themselves admiring the latest prints. The building became the meeting place for the Parisian elite. Artists, writers and intellectuals of all sorts gathered there and discussed the progress of photography: Théophile Gautier, the critic Janin, Gozlan, Préault, Delacroix, Balzac, Chasseriau, Baudelaire, Baron Rothschild. Upon leaving the atelier Bisson, all these celebrities entered Le Gray's studio, where he presented them with free prints, whereafter Bisson did the same. None of them dreamed of billing their working hours.

Such generosity, although a sign of the amateur spirit of these enthusiasts, also reflected their total lack of business sense, and this soon put an end to the adventure. Le Gray was no pure amateur, neither was he a thorough-going professional, but rather both rolled into one. Unfortunately, he lived in materialistic times which were to see the victory of commercialism. Le Gray, typical of the great primitive artists in photography, exemplified both their refined aesthetics and their poor business sense.

In the 1850s Paris swarmed with photographers of little talent, who climbed onto the bandwagon. The public was no longer very interested in lovely pictures of Parisian landscapes, beautiful rural views or architectural splendor. The invention of the calling card by Diséri in 1854 marked the beginning of the industrial age in photography and meant the end for those whose essential preoccupation was aesthetic. In 1859 a disheartened Le Gray left his studio and departed for Egypt. Before him, in 1856, Le Secq, who refused to make any concessions, had ceased his photographic activities. Nègre sought refuge in the Midi.

Portraitists quickly became the gods of the Parisian smart set. Endowed, perhaps, with somewhat less talent than the pioneers of photography who preceded them, they were to enjoy glory and wealth for some time. Paris was at their feet. In the bosom of the bohemian world, it was Nadar who soon occupied a leading place. Nadar was the pseudonym of Gaspard-Félix Tournachon, a journalist and caricaturist. He founded the *Revue comique* and collaborated with the *Journal pour rire* and with the *Charivari*. He studied photography with Camille d'Arnaud, and, in 1853, opened a studio at 133 Rue Saint-Lazare. (His brother Adrien, a student of Le Gray, opened a studio on the Boulevard des Capucines.) Nadar's studio, located on the roof of the building, was equipped with an elevator in which he took photographs of his friends: Vigny, Gautier and Gérard de Nerval (only a few days before the poet committed suicide).

Nadar knew everyone in Paris and his photographs became famous. His portraits were undoubtedly much better than those of most of his colleagues, in part because of their simplicity, but equally because of the depth and sincerity captured in the faces of the people he knew so well. This first period of his career as a photographer was the one that produced his most beautiful work, the naturalistic portraits that excelled in revealing the truth behind the person. But Nadar had another talent: He gathered around him the great personalities of the day—Delacroix, Gustave Doré, Meyerbeer, Sainte-Beuve, Baudelaire, Offenbach—and regularly-organized parties to which the whole of "Bohemia" was invited.

Nadar started to make a lot of money and soon set up an immense studio at 35 Boulevard des Capucines. "Nadar" was affixed to the front of the building in large red letters designed by Antoine Lumiere and illuminated by gaslight. His activities increased: His studio became a veritable portrait factory, and the quality of his pictures rapidly improved.

There was another photographer who equaled and even surpassed Nadar in success and wealth: Disdéri. Amidst the wave of photographers who were starting a career (especially profitable because of the public interest), Disdéri opened a studio in 1852 in the heart of Paris on the Boulevard des Italiens. He soon realized that his colleague's beautiful portraits were far too costly—one hundred francs per shot at Adam Salomon's or Nadar's—and were thus only accessible to relatively well-to-do people. He had a brilliant idea: In 1854 he created the "calling-card portrait," a small photo (9.5 x 5.5 cm) mounted on thin cardboard. A camera specially fitted with twelve lenses made it possible for him to produce as many portraits on a single plate. Thanks to the reduced costs, he was able to offer these little portraits at the ridiculously low price of twenty francs per dozen! Photographs were suddenly affordable and the number of customers multiplied. Disdéri's studio, unique in Paris because of its luxury and elegance, was besieged by endless lines of people. Soon he was the richest photographer in the world; in his studio ninety people produced more than 2000 prints a day! With his lavish apartment, his country houses and his beautiful carriage and horses, he was the talk of Paris. But his downfall was to be as rapid as his rise. A victim of his own invention, which was put to use by other photographers who made prints at an even lower price, Disdéri ended up in poverty.

Nadar also adjusted himself to the new way of doing business, but his purely commercial activities did not fully satisfy him, and he pursued several other preoccupations. Intensely excited about taking photos by artificial light, he descended into the catacombs and the sewers to make the first real photo-essays of underground Paris. These remarkable photos put him back in the limelight, where he stayed for a time because he took a fancy to aeronautics and undertook the first attempts at aerial photography. In 1856, after having conquered many difficulties and spending a fortune, he succeeded in producing the first plate of this kind. On it one can distinguish the avenue in the Bois de Boulogne, the beginnings of the Arc de Triomphe and, in the background, Ternes, Batignolles and Montmartre. Seven years later, 2000 people crowded together on the Champ de Mars to watch the flight of a super balloon, *Géant*. This event had been announced in all the newspapers. Although the first flight had been a relative success, this second one turned into a disaster: Nadar, his whole family and a few friends crashed in Germany and narrowly escaped death.

Etienne Carjat, another photographer of great repute whose pictures often equaled Nadar's best ones, had set up shop in the Rue Lafitte at the back of a garden. There the Paris intelligentsia had reunions, of which Verlaine wrote: "One still remembers those wonderful evenings at the Rue Lafitte, where the first artists of the world were bound to understand each other." Nadar and Carjat also met at the cafés on the boulevard. Centers of intellectual Paris, they abounded in this fashionable district where more and more theaters, restaurants and newspapers appeared.

Another photographer of note was Adam Salomon, an ex-sculptor, whose atelier, frequented by the wealthy Parisian elite, was located in the Rue de la Rochefoucauld in the ninth arrondissement. Within that privileged area, one could find Carjat (Rue Lafitte), Braun (Rue Cadet), Crémieu (Rue Frochot), Liébert (Rue Saint-Lazare), Moulin (Rue de Faubourg-Montmartre), Pierre Petit (Place Cadet), Reutlinger (Boulevard Montmartre) and Vallon de Villeneuve (Rue Bleue)! An astonishing concentration, it was clear proof of the Parisian passion for photography, and especially for portrait pictures. Predictably, photography became a technique subject to industrialization and to a rising capitalist economy.

Paris was in a ferment during the Second Empire. While a triumphant middle-class enjoyed the privileges of being in favor, armies of workmen plowed the land and new factories sprung up everywhere, their cast-iron and steam engines commandeering attention: ironworks, refineries, steelworks, chemical factories. Handwork was done mostly by people from outside the city, from places such as the Basque country, Brittany, the Savoy and Auvergne. A working day was eleven hours long. Social benefits did not yet exist; living conditions in the barracks on the outskirts of Paris were deplorable.

The middle-class, however, had few complaints: Where the July Monarchy had urged the middle-class to put its money in the bank, the Second Empire made it possible for its citizens to invest in industry. Colossal fortunes were built up quickly. It was possible for a rich man to live on his investments all his life, since the state taxed neither his income nor his capital. For these "nouveau riches" and idlers, pleasure was the main occupation. *La Vie Parisienne* by Offenbach cleverly presented the diversions of this new society. The foreign travel, the parties, the courtisans, as well as the magnificence of country houses were the obligatory symbols of a certain standing. In literature, the prevailing taste was ultraconservative. Victor Hugo lived in exile; *Les Châtiments* and *L'Histoire d'un crime* were illegally imported from across the border. In 1857 Flaubert was dragged before the tribunals for *Madame Bovary*; Baudelaire's *Fleurs du Mal* was condemned for being morally offensive. Literary fashion was in the hands of Octave Feuillet, Paul Féval and Ponson du Térrail; visual art was dominated by Vernet, Meisonnier, Bouguereau and Puvis de Chavannes. Indeed, Manet's *Olympia* was made the object of ridicule by the empress herself.

While society was undergoing transformation, the capital also went through a period of disorder. Napoleon III himself marked the map of Paris with colored pencil and started a direct attack. When the prefect Berger refused to "ruin the city," the emperor appealed to the prefect of the Gironde, Baron Haussmann, and the latter executed Napoleon's plans. Doubtless this urbanization left certain positive things to posterity: the gaslights on the city streets, the canalization and distribution of the waters of the Dhuis and the Vanne, the landscaping of the Bois de Boulogne and the Bois de Vincennes, as well as of several other parks. There was also a negative side however, with often useless destruction. Under the bewildered eyes of Parisians, whole streets were broken up and districts disappeared to make way—according to the official propaganda—for a new town. The underlying reasons for this upheaval were all too transparently based on greed. Expropriation compensations allowed the privileged to become rich quickly. Financial speculation on the condemned buildings—Haussmann himself profited handsomely—facilitated the acquisition of scandalous fortunes. Zola reflected on this in his book *La Curée*, and Fernand Bournon wrote: "The person who had bought an old house on a prospective road was able to get a compensation ten times larger than the value of the property."

Old Parisians could no longer recognize their own town. Within twenty years, twenty thousand houses were destroyed and forty thousand constructed. On the Île de la Cité more than ten churches were destroyed. In the Marais dozens of hotels disappeared. The Latin Quarter was ravaged as whole streets were leveled. Laborers and the poor relocated on the northern and southern outskirts, where the rents remained low. The rich began their march westward, where beautiful residential areas were soon under construction.

While much of the city changed or disappeared, and while most photographers thought about opening a studio and making a fortune, one of them, infatuated with Paris and armed with his bellows camera and his collodion plates, sauntered through the old streets, taking pictures not only of monuments, but also, more importantly, of small shops and ordinary, simple streets. Charles Marville succeeded in capturing in his photographs the soul of the city. His pictures offer a profound view of Paris and, ironically, though often devoid of people, possess the richness of a warm humanity. Marville, because of the technical quality of his fawn-colored pictures, as much as for the inestimable value of the testimony they represent, became *the* photographer of the Paris of that period. He loved photographing the old streets just after the rain, when the light was filtered through a still-gray sky and softly caressed the pavement. The plainness of those street scenes gave the photographs a dreamlike quality. Other photography historians have justly written that the Paris of Balzac, Eugène Sue or Zola is recreated before our eyes in these pictures.

Soon dubbed "The photographer of Paris," with a studio on the Boulevard Saint-Jacques, Marville built up an enormous collection. Today it is housed at the Carnavalet Museum, in the historical library of the city of Paris and in the Town Hall. With their warm, luminous tone, his reproductions remain a visual feast and an inexhaustible source of knowledge. The streets and alleys, the markets, the demolition activities—all these were inventoried in the pictures he took between 1855 and 1857. One needs to know how to decipher these informative pictures. A magnifying glass, an essential adjunct, reveals thousands of details of Parisian life at that time. One learns that the price of a restaurant dinner varied between 0,80 francs and 1,50 francs, and an ordinary dinner (beef and broth) cost 30 centimes. A half liter of beer went for 20 centimes, a bath cost 40 centimes in the bath house but 75 centimes at home! *Thérésa* was on at the Alcazar, Paul Féval produced *Le Mari embaumé*, Alexandre Dumas published *Isabelle de Bavière*.

Like Le Gray, Le Secq or Nègre, Marville represents the crème de la crème of a great school of photographers. He possessed a particular concept of photography at a time when most of his colleagues viewed it as nothing more than an industry. The influence of Disdéri and the proliferation of portrait studios radically altered the photographic world. As Gisèle Freund observed: "The manual work and the individual spirit of the beginning of photography disappeared little by little to make place for a more and more impersonal trade." The portrait trend resulted in a quarter of a century of mediocre photography.

Other, less famous photographers did keep aloof from the essentially commercial preoccupations of the majority of the portraitists. Such artists as the count of Aquado, Louis Probert and Victor Regnault continued to work for their own pleasure. And Charles Soulier produced around 1865 some very subtle pictures of the Parisian landscape. Once associated with Chouzard, then with Ferrier, Soulier specialized in stereoscopic views, and with the aid of this process he made some of the first snapshots on the streets of Paris.

The stereoscopic technique, invented in 1852 by the Englishman Brewster, became popular around 1855, but only recently has its role in the development of photography been sufficiently appreciated. The stereoscope seems to have satisfied the public's desire for photographs that could capture human figures in unposed attitudes. Baudelaire attested to its popularity when he wrote in 1859: "Thousands of greedy eyes were directed at the holes of the stereoscope as on the windows of infinity." It had become the latest craze.

In his studio located at Belleville on the Rue Fessart, Jules Richard set up his *Verascope* which, because it had the magic power to restore visual relief and was easy to use, could lend an irresistible charm to stereoscopic photos. After the photograph was developed, it was viewed through stereoscopic reversible binoculars, which created the three-dimensional effect. Other manufacturers, such as Joux, Mockenstein and Gaumont also specialized in stereoscopic material. In 1860 the famous stereoscopic photo series of Paris by Soulier and Ferrier appeared. The *Photographic News* noted the following in May 1861: "Of the thousands of walking people and moving vehicles of all kinds, not a single one is blurred. Even the figures in the shade can be seen perfectly, and in spite of this the exposure does not exceed a fraction of a second. [. . .] ." (These relatively short exposures were obtained thanks to a reduction in the focal distance of the lens in this type of camera.) From 1862 on Hippolyte Jouvin enjoyed an enormous success with his collection of *Vues instantanées de Paris* (snapshots of Paris). It contained more than two hundred shots depicting not only the quays and boulevards, swarming with people, but also events such as the parade of troops on the Pont de la Concorde on August 15, 1862 (the day of Saint Napoléon); and the carnival and festivities in Montmartre and Saint-Cloud. Other stereoscopists, such as Braun and Lamy, now began to offer their lively pictures to the public. These pictures on cardboard or glass, offering a spectacular representation of daily life in France, but also the chance of discovering far-away countries, were available in the millions. With the snapshot—forerunner of the postcard—a new vision, with affinities to Impressionism, was created.

Paris was astir in the late 1860s. In 1867 a new World's Fair was held on the Champ de Mars. In 1869 widespread criticism of the republicans was aimed against Haussmann, followed by stormy elections and the fall of the ministry. Then the "terrible year" of 1870 started. In January barricades were put up at Belleville following Rochefort's arrest. On July 19 France declared war on Prussia. The beginning of September marked the disaster of Sedan when the emperor was captured and imprisoned. On September 4, Gambetta proclaimed the new republic at the Town Hall. And, on September 17 the Prussians, camped at the gates of Paris, surrounded the capital.

Nadar, delighted by the fall of the empire he detested, organized a group of balloonists and established a base near Sainte-Pierre-de-Montmartre. He succeeded in securing aerial contact with the rest of the country with the balloons *Neptune* and *Strasbourg*. The Gare d'Orleans and the Gare du Nord were transformed into workshops for airships. Nadar later acknowledged he had earned a veritable fortune from this affair.

The new year, 1871, began badly as Prussian artillery shells rained down on the city. Paris suffered, and her citizens were hungry and cold. On January 26 the government capitulated; Paris was stupefied by the surrender. The National Assembly, fleeing to Bordeaux, entrusted executive power to Thiers. Shortly thereafter, the rebellion against the government began. On March 26 Paris elected a Commune. The government retreated to Versailles. An egalitarian hope became stronger as a new ideology swept the city. The first proletarian revolution was born, although it lasted only seventy-two days.

Though the events of March 1871 were exceptional, few photographs exist of the turbulent month. In the face of violence and political instability, most photographers reacted in the same way as many other members of the middle and upper classes: They fled Paris for their lives. Nadar, it is true, was in command of a force of airships, and thus was able to take some pictures of the balloon take-off at the beginning of the siege of Paris. Disdéri photographed several bastions, ramparts, the bunkers of Point-de-Jour, that formidable piece of artillery the *Josephine* (the Big Bertha of the age), and then he, too, disappeared. At the beginning of May, Pierre Petit fixed on collodion the destruction of Thiers's house and then vanished. Gone were Franck, Bacal, Reutlinger, Block and Dontenville, to name a few. In all likelihood a great number of them abandoned their studios and equipment and fled toward Versailles. Their exile lasted only a few days, until after the Commune was quashed. Then they surfaced again and took photographs of the ruins still smoking, the gutted houses, the destroyed barricades. With a greed matching their eagerness, they published and sold thousands of photographs, which were snapped up immediately. The bookstores were flooded with calling cards, postcards, prints and books: *Guide Recueil de Paris brûlé* by Pierre Petit; *Siège de Paris 1870–71*, followed by *Ruines de Paris in 1871* by Thiersault; *Ruines de l'Hotel de Ville* by P. Emonts; *Ruines de Paris et ses environs* by Disdéri (a book with an itinerary that carefully avoids the cemetery Père-Lachaise, the barracks of Lobau, and the walls of the Luxembourg, where the bodies of the Communards were piled); *Ruines de Paris* by Liébert (one of the few who took some pictures of the Commune at la Concorde and the Town Hall).

Others went even further. Certain unsavory individuals, whose publications could be called forerunners of the so-called scandal press, did not hesitate to release fake photographs made all the more credible because of the technique employed. Marconi, for example, devised fake photos that purported to show corpses of national guardsmen and children killed by the Prussians. Appert, who also assembled a *Ruines de Paris*, then published *Crimes de la Commune*, a series of photographic montages and collages—an art in which he excelled—which presented dramatic events during the time of the Commune. In these morally questionable works, he made use of authentic portraits of those who played key roles in the events, superimposed over drawings or photos of other people, all of this staged with supreme technical skill. Thus, from the Rue Haxo to Montmartre, from La Roquette to the War Tribunal, these so-called historical documents satisfied the morbid curiosity of many Parisians. All of this "photo journalism" was, without exception, slanted against those who participated in the events of the Commune. Their regrettable acts were highly publicized while the execution of forty thousand Communards at Versailles was ignored. Thus, for the first time, photography was used for purposes of propaganda. It was also the first time that police used photography—in this case, pictures taken on the barricades—to identify and arrest insurrectionists, who were then deported or, more often, executed.

Only a handful of photographers, having understood the witnessing power of photography, dared to leave the comfort of their studios to venture out into the streets during the insurrection: Liébert we have already mentioned; Collard produced several excellent pictures of several barricades, among them the formidable "Château Gaillard" in the Rue Rivoli.

Perhaps the most convincing testimony, produced with a spirit full of curiosity and comprehension, was the work of Bracquehais, considered to be the first real photo-journalist of France. In the midst of all the tumult, he traipsed all over Paris with his heavy camera and tripod. At Porte Maillot, he captured the results of the systematic bombing; in Montmartre, he took several admirable pictures of the famous cannons that belonged to the Commune; in Auteuil and the Pont-Neuf, he photographed the barricades; in the Tuileries, he shot a series on the Versailles troops. But the majority of his pictures (109 plates consigned to the National Library in November 1871) were taken on the Place Vendôme where the general staff was headquartered, among these a wonderful sequence of the fall of the Vondôme column. Bracquehais used these protected locations to photograph a great number of Parisians (and national guardsmen) who came to watch the photographer, knowing that he was, in their eyes, a symbol of the detested empire. The densely populated photos reveal what the Communard spirit was all about: The road worker stands next to the guardsman; the shopkeeper rubs elbows with the barmaid; the eighty-year-old leans on the street urchin. When the bloody week ended, Bracquehais circulated more freely and took pictures of what was left of the civil war: the ruins of the burnt-out buildings, but also the remains of the barricade on the corner of the Boulevard Richard-Lenoir, where Delescluze died. These particular pictures were not used commercially, as were those by others mentioned earlier. Bracquehais made them merely to document the tumultuous period. In less than a few weeks, he managed to paint an astonishing portrait of a fleeting time. His pictures serve as incredible documents of a period and are charged with a life and a pulse formerly unknown.

Paris began to dress her wounds. Thiers established power and the National Assembly adopted a law declaring the "construction of a church on the Montmartre hill" for public use and purpose, as a gesture of thanks to the heavens for saving the city. Thus the Basilique du Sacré-Coeur was built. After 1919, the date of its completion, it dominated Paris with its massive white presence.

The period that followed was a gray and gloomy one for photography. In the capital, the photographers took up their activities again. The mercenary spirit of some infected many of mediocre talent, and hundreds of portrait studios were established. In scientific and artistic circles photography fell into disfavor. The golden age of the calotypists and the great portraitists had come to an end. Nadar moved from the Boulevard des Capucines to a more modest location in the Rue d'Anjou. Carjat's favors for the Commune caused him to lose a large part of his clientele. Although calling cards continued to be a success, Disdéri was ruined by the competition. The portraitist trade soared, and in 1891 it supported more than half a million people! Photography was flourishing commercially but stagnating as an art form.

In Paris regular universal exhibitions took place again. Although photography was recognized as one of liberal arts, technological advances resulted in greatly increased popularity of the genre. The newly constructed Eiffel Tower provoked many abusive articles and petitions, and became the symbol of the Exhibition of 1889. On the other end of the Champ de Mars the huge *Galerie des Machines* was built. Electric lights appeared. The gelatin-bromide plate was invented and spurred renewed interest in photography: Newspapers which had been illustrated with drawings and engravings could now use photographic prints. Already in 1864 the Englishman Woodbury had created photoglyptics, a process of mechanical reproduction that made it possible to obtain prints that were almost as beautiful as the original. From 1873 onward, Paris became enamored of the first magazines that featured wonderful, hand-glued sepia pictures of remarkable finesse. *Paris Theatre* offered its readers a little four-page journal that opened on the portrait of a celebrity. *Le Galerie contemporaine* published the biographies and portraits of all the celebrities of the day and was probably the most influential collection of the period. It featured works by Adam Salomon, Pierre Petit, Carjat, Nadar, Franck and others.

Thanks to the photo-mechanical technology, successfully perfected by Poitevin, the news press was also able to use photography. In his laboratory in the Rue de Faubourg Saint-Jacques, Poitevin invented photo-typogravure. The process was popularized by Gillot, who was the first to start a phototypogravure studio, and by Charles-Guillaume Petit whose invention, simili-gravure, would influence the development of other photographic technology. On September 5, 1886, the *Journal Illustré* published the first photo-reportage: Nadar's interview of the famous chemist Chevreul, illustrated with photographs by Nadar's son, Paul. Two years later, *Le Figaro* printed an interview with General Boulanger, also with pictures by Paul Nadar, taken with one of the first Kodaks (his father owned the sole selling rights for Kodak in France). The first monthly with many photo-illustrations was published in 1876: *Paris Moderne*. It was hailed as "a lively, original series of inestimable documentary value."

Toward the end of the nineteenth century, the world of photography underwent a new transformation. Richard Maddox was at the center of the technical and aesthetic changes that altered the photographic horizon; his invention of the gelatin-bromide plate, improved in 1876 by Charles Harper, made it possible for the industry to start working in shifts. The "dry" plate encouraged the interest of amateur photographers, for whom the equipment was lightened and simplified. Manufacturers competed with each other in ingenuity to attract purchasers of camera equipment. Between 1880 and 1890 the market was flooded with all sorts of portable instruments: countless models of all shapes, some of which were small enough to be concealed in scarves, walking sticks and hats. But the market was dominated by the box camera and binoculars. The streets and parks of Paris filled up with amateur photographers, even more so after the appearance in 1888 of the famous Kodak camera, which was accessible to even modest-income families. "Binoculars," on the other hand, were a middle-class affair. Among these middle-class enthusiasts were some people whom we may justly call great amateurs, some of whom started clubs and societies, and organized exhibitions. While the majority remained unknown, some were familiar names to the public, such as Zola, Degas and Vuillard.

Zola befriended Pierre Petit, Carjat and Nadar, after being introduced to them at the café Gerlois, near the Place Clichy. It was a favorite gathering place of avant-garde painters, who referred to their informal meetings as the *Salon des refusés* (salon of the rejected). With his abundant enthusiasm, Zola photographed all his friends—all of Paris in fact. He strolled in the Tuileries, on the Buttes-Chaumont and down the boulevards; he lingered at the Place Clichy, where he took magnificent pictures in the rain; he dawdled by the Seine, where he captured the tugboats adorned by their own smoke. His plates are essentially snapshots of street life and public places. He was thrilled by the World's Fair of 1900: There he produced hundreds of photos of national buildings and, from the top of the Eiffel Tower, he captured panoramic views from the dizzying heights. Zola was the exemplar of the new type of amateur, shooting Paris and its surroundings during his Sunday walks. His pictures are a reflection of his literary works and his taste for naturalistic subjects. He may have been an amateur, but he had a professional's interest in the technology of photography, which with the new instruments fabricated by Belliéni, Mackenstein and Carpentier was ready to document the arrival of the twentieth century.

The printer Louis Vert, who lived near the Place Bandoyer, left an impressive quantity of glass plates to the Carnavelet Museum and the Société Française de photographie. These plates were produced with the aid of an astounding instrument: the Guido-Sigriste, a small technical marvel that permitted an extraordinary exposure time until then unequaled by a commercial instrument—1/5000 of a second. Vert became *the* observer of street life and has left us countless pictures, often of little-known, turn-of-the-century Paris locales. He apparently learned a lot from Petit, another hunter of picturesque places who took memorable pictures of Les Halles and of the Parisian markets.

Toward the end of the century, an essentially aesthetic movement arose among numerous enlightened amateurs: pictorialism. While the cream of the bourgeoisie and the prestigious laureates of the big exhibitions gathered in the famous Photo-club of Paris, this bohemian group ignored the fashionable salon and dedicated itself to amassing the largest and most important collection of pictures in existence: more than 12,000 plates culled from various public and private sources.

During this period, when so many professionals and amateur photographers were infatuated by the countless new technical possibilities, one particular man stood out. He was to enthrall Paris and make an indelible impression on the history of photography. Eugène Atget's genius was his ability to portray the link between two centuries: He employed a nineteenth-century technique to photograph the end of that century and the beginning of the twentieth. Atget returned to Paris in 1889 after a turbulent life full of personal disasters and frequent changes of vocation. He was a frequent visitor to Montparnasse and became acquainted with the many painters who lived there. After unsuccessful flings with painting and the theater, he decided in 1898 to become a photographer. The sign above the doorway to his studio at 17 Rue Champagne-Première read: *Documents pour artistes*. This referred to his ambition to create a collection of everything artistic and picturesque in the city, and thus began his long and fruitful journeys through the streets of Paris, from which he accumulated plates of façades, old houses, architectural details and rows of streets, but also of people, tradesmen and workmen. More important, he took precious pictures of the small trades that were already disappearing, annihilated by growing industrialization. Using an old 18 x 24 plate instrument, Atget stored up an incredible number of plates of the capital, many of them prints that offered an astonishingly fresh vision. His pictures are marked by an open, frank perspective, and a preoccupation with capturing the truthfulness of the moment. In this quest he shared a common interest with Stieglitz, another forerunner of modern photography. Indeed, they ran into each other during the several weeks when they were both taking pictures of the Boulevard Bonne-Nouvelle near the gate of Saint-Martin.

Unwittingly and for all his humility, Atget proved himself the conjuror of the old Paris. He left us an incomparable iconographic treasure trove. At a time which gave birth to Pictorialism (in essence an esthetic movement), when the celebrated Photo-Club of Paris was attracting the flower of the citizenry and the prestigious prizewinners of the big exhibitions, Atget, a typical Bohemian, far removed from the artistic squabbles of the Salons, dedicated his days to bearing witness and put together a most impressive treasury of pictures. Counting the various collections, there are more than ten million plates, a colossal piece of work, comparable only to that of Cheval in another field.

Among the naturally diverse reasons, overt and covert, for his activities, Atget's love of Paris is incontrovertible; prolific and inspired, this man has understood how to pass on to the world about him a stance which presages the new way of seeing things characteristic of the twentieth century.

Prolific and inspired, Atget managed to convey to the world a way of looking that was to be characteristic of the twentieth century. His great interest in daily things and ordinary people was evident in his photographs of lace and herb salesmen, errand-boys and cab drivers, dog trimmers and merchants, cobblers, butchers, and prostitutes and their pimps. With unflagging passion and equal pleasure, he captured the ragmen and the spectators of Grand Guignol at the Luxembourg. If similar preoccupations also existed in the United States and England, Atget was not aware of them. He labored in total isolation and his work did not become known until long after his death in the years following the end of World War I. It is only fitting that special homage be paid here to his innovating vision, his fresh spirit, his passion for everyday things, and his affection for the people and places of Paris.

The world quickly became engrossed in photography, but, as we have seen, it was in Paris that photography enjoyed its first triumphs, and it was Paris that knew the first great artists of the medium, the calotypists. Those sensitive works have been and are still considered to represent the first flowering of photographic art. It was in Paris that Niepce's invention was first used to document the birth of the industrial age, which was accompanied by the rise of the great portraitists. During the latter part of the century, the Parisian infatuation with photography only deepened: the city had been seduced by this new form of art.

Photography has contributed a great deal to Paris. It has served to record for posterity the proof of the richness of the capital's heritage. Change is inevitable, but the invention of the silver plate—of these pictures that are memory itself—has miraculously permitted us the ephemeral visions of the past. It is in this sense that photography has contributed to the creation of an eternal Paris.

Jean-Claude Gautrand, 1985.

CHAPTER I

THE PARIS OF THE FORERUNNERS

Paris's love affair with photography began at the optician's shop of Charles Chevalier at the westernmost edge of the Île de la Cité, across from the statue of Henry IV. It was there that Niepce met Daguerre and as their friendship blossomed, so did their photographic discoveries. When Niepce departed from the scene prematurely, Daguerre alone was accorded the glory of developing a new reproduction process—the daguerréotype. Parisians were beguiled by the ability of these silvered plates to transfix time. They were indeed magical, these plates that were tantamount to visual diaries, and as soon as the secrets of the process were unveiled, people not only in Paris but around the world were eager to experiment with the camera obscura.

Of the many pictures that were taken at the time, only a few have survived. These delicate images, marked by time with zebra stripes, reflect a Paris unknown to us—the Paris of the 1840s. Some of the plates reveal a city whose medieval roots are still evident in the antiquated aspects of certain neighborhoods. There is something mineral and silent about them; and yet, as the "baby pictures" of photography, they contain a wealth of information. Some of the names of these photographic pioneers are known to us: Fizeau, Bayard, Martens, Hubert, Girault de Pranzy, Richebourg, Nègre and, obviously, Daguerre. With their help, photography would discover its dramatic power to capture fleeting time, and rescue from oblivion "the pendent ruins," in Baudelaire's words, "the precious things, the shape of which will disappear and which demand a place in the archives of our memory. . . ."

Daguerre's achievement cannot be denied, but his process had its drawbacks: the fragility of the plate, the reversed image, the long exposure time and the fact that only a single image could be produced. These factors explain why researchers such as Talbot and Bayard experimented with paper. The new method, baptized "calotype," introduced the "negative-positive" process that is used today in all photography. Thus, calotype represented the beginning of photography as we know it. Although the public favored the dry precision of the daguerréotype over the grainier paper image, the paper process triumphed. It offered much shorter exposure times, multiple prints and, most important, less expensive production costs.

Charles Nègre was among the most brilliant of the early photographers. A student of Delaroche and later of Ingres, this talented painter soon discovered the new art form and even took part in one of the demonstration sessions at the Académie des beaux-arts. Nègre threw himself into photography with unflagging enthusiasm and his work, which has been almost totally preserved, proves the variety of his inspiration and talent. His atelier on the Quai de Bourbon on the Île Saint-Louis was the base from which he hauled his heavy instrument out into the city, day after day. He was the first to use photography to document the everyday life of the streets: the tradespeople, the market scenes on the quais and the small, daily dramas, such as the collapse of a sick horse. He sought to emphasize detail to surpass the simply picturesque. His images testify to this achievement. His pictures are artfully composed, his lighting remarkable. To understand why Nègre occupies a special place in the avant-garde of photographers, one need only compare his work to that of so many other calotypists who were more occupied with bland pictures of landscapes or architecture.

Calotype, with its many practitioners, made it possible for photography to leave a large quantity of precious works to posterity. With the collodion method, created in 1851, increased precision and sensitivity were possible. More and more amateurs were attracted to the pastime of taking pictures. Louis Blanquart-Evrard did his part to popularize this new art by establishing, also in 1851, the first photographic printshop. It produced the first books illustrated with photographs, which were glued in by hand. Two of those books, *Mélanges photographiques*, and *Le Paris photographique*, reproduce a number of pictures in which Paris itself is the subject. Many of these pictures were taken by such masters as Le Secq, Le Gray, Baldus, Bayard, Disdéri, Fortier, Ducamp, Durandelle and Marville.

Among the earliest photographers of Paris, another name that deserves special attention is Charles Marville. Between 1851 and 1879, he produced the most complete and extraordinary body of work—a diary of Paris as it changed drastically under Baron Haussmann's initiative. Marville's work is interesting for two reasons: His pictures reveal a stunning sense of light—many of them were taken after it had rained—and they contain information that teaches us a lot about Parisian life during the nineteenth century. More than 800 plates and three nearly-complete collections of Marville's work compose a rich inventory of the streets and houses of the city. He is known as "the photographer of Paris," but his pictures contain none of the picturesque qualities that the title suggests. Instead, the photographs are stark and unsentimental. Working in a systematic way, Marville followed closely the demolition works directed by Haussmann. For example, he made an exhaustive pictorial study of the work done on the Avenue de l'Opéra. But his pictures go beyond documentation; they have an added dimension that elevates them to greatness. They earn such lofty praise in bearing witness to a vanished heritage. Also, they provide visual proof for what Jules Ferry has called the "fantastic tales of Baron Haussmann."

Daguerre, Nègre, Marville and their contemporaries serve as guides to a Paris that once existed but is no more. Their pictures reveal to us marvelous old buildings that have disappeared and interesting architectural details—the pump of the Notre-Dame, for example—that have changed over the years. They point out to us the old medieval streets—Pirouette, Traversiere, Neuve-Notre-Dame, de la Tonnelerie. They show us the river Bièvre that, before becoming a nauseating sewer, Benserade described as "a beautiful little stream with running, whistling water." They introduce us to sleepy courtyards, old bridges, vanished neighborhoods and suburbs. Thanks to the magic of all these sepia pictures, the Paris of Balzac, Baudelaire and Eugène Sue is revived before our eyes.

PARIS ON DAGUERRÉOTYPE

1. *The Flore Pavilion. 1839.* Louis-Jacques Mandé Daguerre (Conservatoire des arts et métiers). First proof produced by Daguerre before the members of the Académie des beaux-arts. Thanks to this new way of reproduction, "the smallest details, the outlines of buildings and the earth . . . appear with an incredible precision," said the *Journal of the Franklin Institute* in 1839.

Here, at the southwestern corner of the Old Louvre, rises the Flore Pavilion adjacent to the Pont-Royal and bordering the Tuileries Gardens.

2. *Bank of the Seine, 1840/1844.* Hossard (Musée d'Orsay). A daguerréotype of a series done by Hossard (professor at the School of Polytechnics and a friend of Daguerre's) of the banks of the Seine. The Kodak Foundation recently donated the series to the Musée d'Orsay.

3. *The Île de la Cité, ca. 1845.* Mauban (La Société française de photographie). Oxydized and marked by time, this daguerréotype testifies to the Parisian landscape of the Cité before the Haussmann demolition. In the foreground is the Quai des Grands-Augustins.

On the Seine, the washing-places where, close together on their knees, washerwomen beat and scoured their linen. To the right of Notre-Dame is the old Hôtel-Dieu, connected with the Left Bank by the Pont Saint-Charles (now gone). In the foreground is the old Petit Pont.

In 1833 Corot had painted exactly the same view, entitled "Notre-Dame et le quai des Orfèvres" (Carnavelet Museum).

4. *The Louvre and the Pont-Neuf, 1848.* Anonymous (La Société française de photographie). On the bridge, note some of the twenty shops built into the arches. For a long time they were mainly used to sell toys.

5. *View of Paris, 1842.* Friedrich von Martens (La Bibliothèque nationale). View of the Pont-Neuf, the Vert-Galant, the Île de la Cité and the Quai de l'Horloge.

6. *View of Paris, 1842.* Friedrich von Martens (Conservatoire des arts et métiers). The view from the towers of Notre-Dame includes, from right to left, the tower of Saint-Jacques, Town Hall, the Church of Saint-Germain and the first

Pont Louis-Philippe, which was demolished in 1860.

These two daguerréotypes were made on a panoramic instrument devised by Martens. He used curved plates that could cover an angle of about 150 degrees. The lens pivoted thanks to a crank-driven mechanism. These two shots are, like many daguerréotypes, reversed to make them more realistic.

7. *Notre-Dame and the Île de la Cité, 1838.* Louis-Jacques Mandé Daguerre (Museum of Austin, Texas).

8. *Boulevard, 1839.* Louis-Jacques Mandé Daguerre (George Eastman House). Plates 7 and 8 were two of the first daguerréotypes made in Paris by Daguerre himself. The first one, which needs to be reversed, was taken on the Pont de la Tournelle. To the left is the Pont Louis-Philippe. It affords a rare view of the medieval Parisian skyline that had been largely unchanged since 1300.

The second of these daguerréotypes was sent to the King of Bavaria by Daguerre personally. The original was destroyed during the bombing of Munich in World War II. It is the first photographic print of human figures. The two silhouettes by the side of the boulevard are a bootblack and his client.

9. *The Guard in the Courtyard of the Tuileries, 1842/1848.* Anonymous (La Société française de photographie). Improvements made to the Daguerre process soon allowed the taking of genre pictures. The exposure time was reduced from a quarter of an hour to fifteen seconds, and in 1843 to just a few seconds.

THE PARIS OF CHARLES NÈGRE

10. *View of Paris, 1852.* Taken from the top of the Church of Saint-Gervais, with Town Hall in the foreground. One can also distinguish the Conciergerie, the Sainte-Chapelle and the first Pont Louis-Philippe. The picture was made from a heliographic engraving with black ink.

11. *Eastern Façade of Notre-Dame, 1853.* Print on salted paper from a paper negative (Nègre family collection). At the foot of Notre-Dame, the scaffolding by the central portal indicates the beginning of restoration work on the cathedral by Viollet-le-Duc.

12. *The Gargoyle, 1853*. Print on salted paper from a waxed paper negative (National Gallery of Canada, Ottawa). One of Nègre's strongest pictures: a portrait of his photographer friend Henri Le Secq on the northern walk of Notre-Dame. Inspired by the engraving of their friend Merryon, this photograph superbly emphasizes the stone lacework of the vertical walls, the astonishing gargoyle and, at the foot of the tower, the old houses that were destroyed by Haussmann.

13. *The Little Chimney Sweeps, 1851*. Waxed paper negative, printed on albumenized paper (National Gallery of Canada, Ottawa). Taken on the Quai Bourbon close to Nègre's residence, this photo was probably staged, yet has a remarkable sense of realism.

Nègre's background as a painter explains his penchant for genre pictures. It undoubtedly also explains the subtle use of the process "paper negative" to obtain the grainy texture of this print. The fading distance, the use of light, the search for expression in movement—all this made Charles Nègre one of the first to explore the aesthetics of photography and to capture its essence. These scenes, so much like Daumier (another resident of the Île Saint-Louis), prompted C. Bauchal, journalist of *La Lumière* (the first French magazine on photography, published from 1851 on), to write this review:

There go these three gloomy winter birds, casting to the wind their monotonous look that announces the hard season. . . . They casually follow the gray parapet of one of our quais where the setting sun stretches and cuts out their shadows. Murillo is completely captured in this naïve, picturesque and striking scene.

14. *Pifferari in Paris, 1853*. Albumenized paper from a collodion negative (La Société française de photographie). Photographed in the yard at 21 Quai de Bourbon, these traveling young musicians, who walked the streets of Paris, belonged to the Parisian scene of the 1850s. Here, again, Charles Nègre managed to lend a natural look to his charming composition.

15. *Market Scene on the Pont de l'Hôtel-de-Ville, 1851/52*. Paper negative, printed on salted paper (Nègre family collection). The low sensitivity of this process and the rudimentary character of the lenses cause the blurring, a fault which lends the picture, one of the first snapshots in the history of photography, a surprising dynamism. Charles Nègre also made a painting of this scene, which was exhibited at the Salon of 1850.

16. *The Fall of a Horse, 1855/60*. Albumenized print of a collodion negative (Galerie Octant, Paris). A real snapshot, made possible by the use of collodion (1851), which was more sensitive than negative paper, and the use of a stereoscopic instrument, perfected in 1844. The location is the Quai Bourbon.

17. *Organ-Grinder from Barbarie, before 1853*. Salted paper, from a waxed-paper negative (Nègre family collection). Made in Charles Nègre's yard, this scene presents one of the typical street characters of Paris. (A painted print of it was exhibited at the Salon of 1853.) The number of these organ-grinders grew so rapidly that the citizens of Paris protested, and as a result of a decree in 1860 it was forbidden to play on the street. The photograph expressed Nègre's astonishing ability to capture the subtle meaning of a scene. Ernest Lacan explains:

There is a strange contrast between the attentive pose, the marvelous physiognomy of these children who have seen so little and who are surprised by everything, and the expression of lassitude and discouragement of the old traveling musician who has seen so much himself.

18. *Cocoa Vendor, 1853* (Nègre family collection). Another typical street character, the cocoa vendor—here with his drinking fountain—who frequented public parks to the joy of the children and the adults.

> *Here is the musical cocoa vendor,*
> *armed with his golden taps;—*
> *his taps are snakes*
> *from which his cocoa splashes*
> *into the mugs of the children.*
> (Paul Fort, *Ballades françaises*)

THE PARIS OF CHARLES MARVILLE

19. *Square and Church of Saint-Germaine-l'Auxerrois, ca. 1852*. Calotype (La Bibliothèque historique de la Ville de Paris). A church that has witnessed the vicissitudes of history. The first church was built in the seventh century, destroyed by the Normans in 886, then reconstructed in the year 1000; it was renovated in the thirteenth century in Gothic style (central portal, choir), in the fifteenth century in a flamboyant style (porch, nave, transept) and in the sixteenth century in Renaissance style (chapel, lateral portals); in the eighteenth century it was ravaged and then transformed during the Revolution into a forage warehouse. Given back to

worship under the empire, it was ransacked after the events of July 1830, transformed into an annex of Town Hall in 1838 and then restored to a church in 1855. The Gothic tower and the adjacent Town Hall were built in 1859 to fill up empty space left after the Haussmann demolition. Hugo has compared the general effect to a giant oil and vinegar set—the tower being the handle and the two buildings the cruets. On the square circus people gave performances.

20. *The Alley of the Try-Outs, 1865.* This street owes its name to the fact that people who had bought horses, donkeys and mules tried them out here. The horse market disappeared after the Boulevard Saint-Michel was constructed.

This wasn't the countryside, for there were houses and streets; it wasn't a city, for the streets were tracks like country roads, with weeds growing; it wasn't a village, for the houses were too high. What was it then? It was an inhabited place with no one in it, a deserted spot with a few people, a boulevard of a large city, a street in Paris, wilder than the night in a forest, gloomier than a cemetery in the daytime. This was the old quarter, where the horse market was.
(Victor Hugo, Les Misérables.)

21. *Passage du Dragon, ca. 1860* (Carnavalet). This courtyard, connecting the Rue de Rennes with the Rue du Dragon, dated from the eighteenth century. It functioned as the artisans' own little city, with a life of its own.

22. *Rue Traversione leading to the Sainte-Geneviève Hill, ca. 1858.* This street disappeared when the Rue Monge was constructed. With its uneven cobblestones, its gutters in the middle of the street, its stones for protecting houses against cart-wheels, it recalls medieval Paris, the Paris of Balzac and his *Comédie Humaine.*

23. *Crossroads of the Rue des Prairies and the Rue des Rondeaux, ca. 1870* (La Bibliothèque historique de la Ville de Paris). The Rue des Prairies and the Rue des Rondeaux ran alongside the Cemetery of Père Lachaise. Where the streets met (near the present Place Gambetta), there is a family gathered around a garden table, illustrating life in the Parisian countryside around 1850.

24. *Rue Vieille Notre-Dame, ca. 1868.* Opened in 1603, this street once connected the Rue Censier with the Rue Daubenton. Today it is part of the Rue de la Clef.

25. *Old Town Hall and the Old Pont d'Arcole, 1852.* Calotype (Carnavalet). The old Pont d'Arcole, then a suspension bridge, was replaced in 1854 by the present one. Behind it is the Place de Grève and Town Hall before the fire of 1871. The present Town Hall was built in Renaissance style in 1873.

On the Place de Grève, workmen used to assemble when they were on strike. The square was also the scene of public executions, which attracted enormous crowds. Philippe and Gaultier d'Aunay, the lovers of the princesses of Bourgogne (1314), Ravaillac (1610), the Marquis de Brinvilliers (1676) and Cartouche (1721) were among those executed here. Also on this spot the four sergeants of La Rochelle were guillotined.

26. *Moving the Palmier Fountain, Place du Châtelet, April 21, 1858.* (La Bibliothèque historique de la Ville de Paris). The fountain was erected in 1808 in the center of the first Place du Châtelet. When the square was enlarged during the Second Empire, the whole column, weighing twenty-four tons, was put on rails and placed about a dozen meters westward to be installed in its present location.

27. *Cours de Bièvre, ca. 1860.* (La Bibliothèque historique de la Ville de Paris).

28. *La Bièvre below the Avenue des Gobelins, ca. 1860* (La Bibliothèque historique de la Ville de Paris). In Roman times a clear river with willows along its banks, the Bièvre entered Paris at the Gate of the Poplars. Then it split into two streams, that flowed together again along the Jardin des Plantes; it ended up in the Seine near the Pont d'Austerlitz. Under the reign of Louis XIV there were refreshment places and renowned brasseries on its banks: The beer of the Gobelins was famous and on Sundays, people crowded together on the green riverbanks where there was still crayfish to be caught. Victim of the tanneries and the dye factories that were built in the seventeenth century, the river became so polluted and unhealthy that it was covered up in 1910.

Also the Bièvre, with its desperate attitude and look of suffering, charmed me more than any other, and I consider the collapse of its valleys and trees an outrage: We had nothing left but this sad countryside, this battered river, these ragged plains, and they are going to be carved up (Huysmans, Croquis parisiens).

29. *The Rue du Passage Saint-Louis, ca. 1870.* (La Bibliothèque historique de la Ville de

Paris). Today, the Rue Champlain near the Rue Ménilmontant; in 1870, the "zone," was inhabited by migrant workers from the provinces—Creusois, Brittons, Savoyards—as well as by Parisians who had been dislocated by demolition work going on in the city.

30. *Horse Market, ca. 1865* (Carnavalet). Founded in 1687, and located near the Rue Geoffroy-Saint-Hilaire, it was at this market (for horses, but also for donkeys, pigs, dogs and other animals) that the strappado torture was inflicted, until Louis XVI suppressed the practice in 1776.

31, 32. *Digging on the Avenue de l'Opéra (Site of the Butte des Moulins), 1876/77* (Carnavalet). The Hill of the Mills was built in the fourteenth century with rubbish and dirt from the various fortification works around Paris. Until the end of the seventeenth century this was a neighborhood of sordid shanties and gambling dens. Then the hill was leveled again and the earth was transported to the Champ-de-Mars.

I had undertaken a voyage not so long but more dangerous than a tour around the world: I went from the Passage Choiseul to the Théâtre-Français by way of the Butte des Moulins. . . . In front, in back, to the right, to the left, everywhere the rubble was tumbling down with a thunderous noise and dust clouds obscured the sky; the workmen didn't give warning and bran-

dished long slats; cartloads of rubbish crossed the valley through hills of debris; the earth trembled; it rained rubble and bricks (Edmond About, Paris Guide).

33. *Digging on the Avenue de l'Opéra at Argenteuil, 1876* (Carnavelet).

34. *The First Demolition Works at the Avenue de l'Opéra, 1876/77* (La Bibliothèque historique de la Ville de Paris). An astonishing photo essay on the demolition of Paris ordered by Baron Haussmann. This savage reconstruction consisted, according to Zola, of "the hacking with a sword at Paris, its veins open and bleeding" (*Curée*). It also destroyed the *Quartier Latin,* the Quartier Antin and Les Halles. Here we see the work on the Butte des Moulins between what are now the Opéra and the Théâtre Français. In the background is the Opéra, built by Charles Garnier between 1862 and 1875.

Paris changes! but nothing in my melancholy has stirred! new palaces, scaffolding, blocks, old districts, everything became for me an allegory and my dear old souvenirs are no more than rocks. (Baudelaire, "Le Cygne"—Les Fleurs du mal)

35. *Place de la Bourse, ca. 1866* (La Bibliothèque historique de la Ville de Paris). The station for coaches and buses in front of the first Vaudeville theater (demolished in 1868, during the construction of the Rue du Quatre-Septembre).

1. Louis-Jacques Mandé Daguerre, 1839.

2. Hossard, 1840/1844.

3. Mauban, ca. 1845.

4. Anonyme / Anonymous, 1848.

5. Friedrich von Martens, 1842.

6. Friedrich von Martens, 1842.

7. Louis-Jacques Mandé Daguerre, 1838.

8. Louis-Jacques Mandé Daguerre, 1839.

9. Anonyme / Anonymous. 1842/1848.

10. Charles Nègre, 1852.

11, 12. Charles Nègre, 1853.

13. Charles Nègre, 1851.

14. Charles Nègre, 1853.

15. Charles Nègre, 1851/1852.

16. Charles Nègre, 1855/1860.

17. Charles Nègre, ca. 1852.

18. Charles Nègre, 1853.

19. Charles Marville, ca. 1852.

20. Charles Marville, 1865. ▶

21. Charles Marville, ca. 1860.

22. Charles Marville, ca. 1858.

23. Charles Marville, ca. 1870.

24. Charles Marville, ca. 1868.

25. Charles Marville, 1852.

26. Charles Marville, 21 avril 1858.

27. Charles Marville, ca. 1860.

28. Charles Marville, ca. 1860.

29. Charles Marville, ca. 1865.

30. Charles Marville, ca. 1870.

31, 32. Charles Marville, 1876/1877.

33, 34. Charles Marville, 1876/1877.

35. Charles Marville, ca. 1866.

CHAPTER II

ATGET AND THE OLD PARIS

Of all the photographers of Paris, Atget is perhaps the best known. Having tried without success to become an actor and a painter, Atget decided in 1898 to supply the painters of Montparnasse with the photographs they needed for their documentation. He was forty-one years old, but he learned quickly, and within a few years he had mastered his craft. He then set to work amassing an ambitious photo collection of everything that was artistic and picturesque about Paris and its surroundings.

Atget often rose at dawn to take advantage of the transparent early-morning light as well as to avoid the morning traffic. He wandered everywhere around Paris, stooped under the weight of the heavy equipment that was essential to his art: a cumbersome bellows camera, a heavy wooden tripod and two or three boxes with glass plates. Every afternoon he developed the pictures he had taken on printing frames installed in his fifth-floor studio in the Rue Campagne-Première. Using specially toned paper, he obtained pictures with a reddish-brown tint. Although this was, in fact, an old-fashioned nineteenth-century technique, it helped Atget establish himself as a twentieth-century photographer.

He chose to photograph realistic scenes of shopkeepers, laborers and peddlers, taking pictures anonymously under his large black cloth, in every corner of the city. With the finished prints, Atget regularly made the rounds of the studios in the Rue Bonaparte, Rue Campagne-Première and Rue Vercingétorix to offer his pictures to such clients as Dunoyer de Segonzac, Braque, de Vlaminck, Foujita, Duchamp, Picasso and Man Ray. He also sold series of his photographs to various cultural institutions in the city: the National Library, the Carnavalet, the Institute of Decorative Arts, the Louvre. Over a period of twenty years, the photographer built up a huge collection of pictures that showed both the old Paris and the new. Unfortunately, his talent remained unrecognized during his lifetime. He died in 1927, completely unknown and practically penniless. Only when the American photographer, Berenice Abbott (an assistant at the time to Atget's neighbor Man Ray), fell in love with his work did his large oeuvre come to light again. After Atget's death, Abbott acquired part of his archives—presently at the Museum of Modern Art in New York—and when she returned to the U.S., she did everything she could to emphasize the importance of his exceptional work. Before long, he was recognized, with Stieglitz, as a founding father of modern photography.

Determined to neglect nothing, to hide nothing from the truth, Atget conducted an astonishing, Proustian investigation. Needless to say, we have a different point of view and we see in his work a liveliness, a dimension and a content that he himself never dreamed of. But with this purity of vision, his work paid homage to the people and places of the past, and it did so with unparalleled technique. Thus, the work is of enormous importance, aesthetically and historically. His city landscapes, his frontal shots of shop windows with blurred, ghostly images of people, his quiet, cobblestoned streets full of atmosphere: They bring to us, elegiacally, the Paris of the beginning of the century.

In the pages that follow, the emphasis is on the photos of tradespeople whom Atget found so engrossing. The colorful people in these pictures recall the subjects of Bouchardon's and Boucher's drawings of the "Cris de Paris," and of characters described by Proust in *La Prisonnière*. These humble street people, with their quaint and unusual trades, brought to the streets of Paris a warmth that no longer exists. The industrial revolution and the birth of a modern economy annihilated this kind of trade. But thanks to Atget's camera, these age-old traditions will be remembered.

THE OLD PARIS

36. *Hôtel de Nantes, 1850.* Anonymous (Carnavalet). Until the middle of the nineteenth century, the Place du Carrousel was situated in a district of old winding streets. In the middle of the square stood the Hôtel de Nantes, where Stendhal died. This daguerréotype was given to M. Berger, prefect of Paris before Haussmann.

37. *The Gare d'Austerlitz, ca. 1869.* Anonymous (La Bibliothèque nationale). Originally this was the platform for the trains of the Paris-Orléans line. Built in 1838, the station was reconstructed by the architect Renault in 1867.

38. *Quai des Grands-Augustins.* Ferrier and Soulier, Stereoscope (Angel Sirot collection). The first quai in Paris was constructed in 1313 to allow Philippe le Bel to travel easily from his palace in the city to his Hôtel de Nesles. This stereoscopic view of the Quai des Grands-Augustins offers a look at daily life during the Second Empire. On the lower level a woman is selling sweetmeats; on the parapets are the stands of shopkeepers who were not yet allowed to have a store in their residences; in the background is the Pont-Neuf and the Louvre.

39. *Panoramic View from the Tower of Saint Jacques, ca. 1860.* Ferrier and Soulier, Stereoscope (Viollet collection). The demolition works had already dug trenches at the edges of the Île Saint-Louis (left) and the Île de la Cité (right), indicating the tracks of the future Pont Louis-Philippe. The old suspension bridge (of the same name) was razed several months later. The Pont Rouge, which connected both islands, was also destroyed, to be replaced by the Pont Saint-Louis.

40, 41. *Panorama of Paris, 1867.* Gueuvin and Bonoldi (La Société française de photographie). Two panoramic views taken from the Tower of Saint-Jacques with the aid of a special camera developed by Koch. They show remarkable views of the center of Paris: The first one shows the area of the Pont Marie, and the Pont de la Tournelle and the Pont au Change; the second one is of an area from Notre-Dame to the Pont des Arts. The effect of Haussmann's work can be seen in these photographs: One can distinguish the excavation work on the spot where, between 1868 and 1878, the new Hôtel de Dieu, the Tribunal de Commerce and the police headquarters were erected.

42. *Panoramic View of the Île de la Cité, ca. 1864.* Edouard-Denis Baldus (Bibliothèque nationale). Magnificent view of the baths of la Samaritaine, the swimming schools and public washing places (of which there were so many along the Seine at that time), the Pont-Neuf, the Conciergerie, Sainte-Chapelle and Notre-Dame. The luxurious Deligny baths, with their 350 cabins, are also visible.

43. *Waterpump of Notre-Dame, 1853.* Henri Le Secq (La Bibliothèque historique de la Ville de Paris). Constructed on the pile-foundation of an old wheat mill and consisting of two suction pumps and force pumps, the pump building was constructed in 1671 to supply some twenty fountains in Paris. At that time, the city used the waters of the l'Ourcq, the Seine and several wells for drinking water. It was destroyed in 1856. In the background is the Quai de Gesvres and the Church of Saint-Gervais.

44. *The Vert-Galant near the Quai des Écoles.* Louis-Désiré Blanquart-Evrard (La Bibliothèque nationale). One can distinguish, across from the statue of the Vert-Galant, the shop of the famous optician Chevalier, who supplied Niepce and Daguerre with photographic equipment.

45. *The Corner of the Rue Mondétour and the Rue Pirouette, 1866.* Louis Jarre (La Bibliothèque historique de la Ville de Paris). Constructed in 1250, the Rue Pirouette disappeared when Baltard's Halles were built. It was in the Rue Mondétour, during the riot of June 1832, that the child who was to be immortalized by Victor Hugo under the name of Gavroche was killed.

46. *Turret on the Place de l'Hôtel-de-Ville, 1852.* Henri Le Secq (La Bibliothèque historique de la Ville de Paris).

The old Paris is no more the shape of the city changes more quickly! than the heart of a mortal being.
(Baudelaire, "Le Cygne," Les Fleurs du Mal)

47. *Passing through the Gate, 1855.* August Bertsch (La Société française de photographie). Print made by Bertsch to prove to the members of the Société française de photographie that he was able to take pictures using an exposure time of a quarter of a second. This photo shows the Gate of Blanche: Merchandise had to be taken into the city by way of one of forty-five gates—each of a different design by the architect Ledoux. The goods were taxed at these

gates, hence the famous verse: "Ce mur murant Paris rend Paris murmurant" (This wall walling Paris has Paris grumbling.)

One is stalled for a long time at the gate, for the egg-merchants, the wagoners and a herd of sheep are in one's way. The sentry, with his hat in his hands, walks back and forth in front of his box to keep warm. The tax commissioner climbs onto the top. . . . (Gustave Flaubert, L'Education sentimentale*).*

48. *Flanders Gate, 1859* Gouviot (La Bibliothèque de la Ville de Paris). At the beginning of the road to Flanders, the architect Ledoux built a rotunda and two pavilions that were used for concession rights and later served as a barracks and as a salt warehouse. Today they are historical landmarks.

THE PARIS OF EUGÈNE ATGET

49. *Street Singers, 1898/1900* (La Bibliothèque historique de la Ville de Paris).

50. *Herb Salesman, 1898* (Carnavalet). This young herb salesman was photographed, like so many of Atget's studies of small tradesmen on the Place Saint-Médard, located at the end of the Rue Mouffetard.

51. *Guignol at the Luxembourg, 1898/1900* (La Bibliothèque historique de la Ville de Paris).

52. *Umbrella Vendor, 1898/1900* (La Bibliothèque historique de la Ville de Paris).

53. *Lace Vendor, 1898* (La Bibliothèque nationale).

54. *Basket Salesman, 1899* (Carnavalet).

55. *Fishmonger, 1899* (Carnavalet).

56. *Nougat Vendor, 1898/1900* (Carnavalet).

57. *Baker, 1898* (La Bibliothèque nationale).

58. *Bread Carrier, 1898* (La Bibliothèque nationale).

59. *Commissioner, 1898* (La Bibliothèque nationale).

60. *Herb Merchants, 1899* (Carnavalet).

61. *Lampshade Merchants, Rue Lepic, 1899* (Carnavalet).

62. *Ragman, Avenue des Gobelins, 1901* (Carnavalet).

63. *Dog Trimmer, 1898* (La Bibliothèque de la Ville de Paris).

64. *Street Paver, 1898* (La Bibliothèque nationale).

65. *Shed of the Golden Compass Inn, Rue Montorqueil, ca. 1905* (La Caisse nationale des monuments historiques). Old inn of the sixteenth century, demolished in 1925. Station post for coaches to Dreux and Creil. In this courtyard in 1938, Lacenaire and his accomplice Avril assassinated a boy who collected entrance money, as was shown in the film *Les Enfants du paradis.*

66. *Cabaret under the Signboard of the Child Bacchus, 1910/1912* (La Caisse nationale des monuments historiques). Located at 61 Rue Saint-Louis-en-Île.

67. *Cabaret under the Sign of the Armed Man, ca. 1910* (La Caisse nationale des monuments historiques). Located at 25 Rue des Blancs-Manteaux.

68. *Cabaret under the Sign of the Drum, 1908* (La Caisse nationale des monuments historiques). 63 Quai de la Tournelle.

69. *Cabaret under the Sign of the Doe, 1904/ 1906* (La Caisse nationale des monuments historiques). 35 Rue Geoffroy-Saint-Hilaire.

70. *Rue Saint-Jacques, ca. 1920* (La Caisse nationale des monuments historiques). The Rue Saint-Jacques near Saint-Séverin. The Rue Saint-Jacques was originally the principal Roman route to Lutèce.

71. *Rue des Ursins, 1923* (La Caisse nationale des monuments historiques). Old Street on the Île de la Cité.

72. *Rue Saint-Rustique, March 1922* (Private collection). Street in Montmartre that dates from the tenth century.

36. Anonyme / Anonymous, 1850.

ymous, ca. 1869.

38. Ferrier et Soulier, ca. 1860.

39. Ferrier et Soulier, ca. 1860.

40, 41. Gueuvin et Bonoldi, 1867.

42. Edouard-Denis Baldus, ca. 1864.

43. Henri Le Secq, 1853.

44. Louis-Désiré Blanquart-Evrard, 1851/1855.

45. Louis Jarre, 1866.

46. Henri Le Secq, 1852.

47. August Bertsch, 1855.

48. Gouviot, 1859.

50. Eugène Atget, 1898.

51. Eugène Atget, 1898/1900.

52. Eugène Atget, 1898/1900.

53. Eugène Atget, 1898.

54. Eugène Atget, 1899.

55. Eugène Atget, 1899.

56. Eugène Atget, 1898/1900.

57. Eugène Atget, 1898.

58. Eugène Atget, 1898.

59. Eugène Atget, 1898.

60. Eugène Atget, 1899.

61. Eugène Atget, 1899.

62. Eugène Atget, 1901.

63. Eugène Atget, 1898.

64. Eugène Atget, 1898.

65. Eugène Atget, ca. 1905.

66. Eugène Atget, 1910/1912.

67. Eugène Atget, ca. 1910.

68. Eugène Atget, 1908.

69. Eugène Atget, 1904/1906.

70. Eugène Atget, ca. 1920.

71. Eugène Atget, 1923.

72. Eugène Atget, 1922.

CHAPTER III

THE SEINE

Paris was born in the middle of the Seine River on the small island now known as the Île de la Cité. The Parisii, a Celtic tribe, took refuge there from invading barbarians during primitive times. They were displaced in 52 B.C. by the Roman legions of Julius Caesar. There at the intersection of the Seine and the dirt road leading north to Flanders and south to Spain, Caesar established the Roman town of Lutèce.

During the fourth century, the Roman Emperors Julian and Valentinian installed on the island an imperial court and a palace on the spot where now stands the Palais de Justice. Five centuries later, the Normans destroyed everything that stood in their way, except the Île de la Cité. Its population, led by Count Eudes, hid behind the great, protective walls and successfully endured a siege that lasted two years.

Under the reign of the Capetians, the city was renamed Paris and burgeoned so that it sprawled over both banks of the Seine—the river functioning as an economic artery. The bridges came next—they number thirty-one today—spanning the river with their immeasurable charm and evocative names: The Pont Louis-Philippe introduces visitors to the architectural richness of the Île Saint-Louis; The Pont-Neuf leads to the heart of Paris and the Île de la Cité; Pont des Arts directs sightseers to the Louvre, the Tuileries or the Gare d'Orsay.

From the Quais d'Ivry and Bercy to Quai Javel, with the rhythm of some of the thirty-one bridges which bestride the river, this unique and diverse landscape plays on its diversity to augment the sources of interest. At the Pont de Tolbiac: Bercy and its wine warehouses, an enclave of times past, well-buried under the age-old planer trees of the old Chateau de Bercy; from the Pont Sully to the Pont Louis-Philippe: the architectural riches of the Île Saint-Louis; from the bridges of the Archbishopric and Louis-Philippe to Pont-Neuf: the heart of Paris with the Cité and its flamboyant chefs-d'oeuvres; from the poetic Pont des Arts up to the Pont de la Concorde: the royal perspectives of the Louvres, the Tuileries, the Institut and the fabulous Gare d'Orsay. From the Invalides, Alexandre-III and l'Alma bridges: the more recent districts, at once more ostentatious and bourgeois, bounded by the fountains of Chaillot and dominated by the proud Eiffel Tower. And it is after the Pont Mirabeau, the praises of which were sung by Apollinaire, that the Seine, before leaving Paris, goes off in cozy search of the last fiery rays of the setting sun.

Today, the tugboats have deserted the river and automobiles have devoured many miles of its embankment. The space has been cut up and dammed in, but the Seine still offers a taste of paradise for dawdling pedestrians. From the upper quais to the shady low embankments, from the Pont de Tobiac to the Pont Mirabeau, over the whole length of this picturesque river, there is an abundance of places to stroll and dream. The photographs of the Seine—of its bridges and boats and people—testify to the river's enduring beauty.

73. *The Point of Vert-Galant, 1945.* Emmanuel Sougez (La Bibliothèque nationale). The willow of Vert-Galant was planted as a cynosure at the western boundary of "Lutèce":

That is what the city of the Parisiens is called in Gallic. It occupies an island in the middle of the river and is connected to both banks by wooden bridges. The river rarely rises or falls: It is the same in summer as in winter; one likes to drink the pure and beautifully clear water (Julian the Apostate, Roman emperor around A.D. 360).

74. *The Île de la Cité, 1961.* Henri Cartier-Bresson. Across from the Pont des Arts, the most beautiful panorama of Paris unfolds, from one side of the river to the other. Snugly enveloped by a silent fog, the Île de la Cité throws its moorings to the two banks of the capital and hides behind the square of Vert Galant, with its wonderful foliage, and the Place Dauphine, with its beautiful seventeenth-century houses. From the Pont des Arts, a magnificent view meets one's eyes—a masterpiece of simplicity, equilibrium and serenity. Artists never tire of this view, nor do passers-by: They know they are contemplating a landscape of true perfection.

75. *View of the Seine and the Île de la Cité, 1950.* René-Jacques.

76. *View of the Île Saint-Louis, 1938.* René-Jacques. The Parisian landscape viewed from one of the most prestigious and oldest restaurants of the capital: La Tour d'Argent. This famous restaurant, a monument to gastronomy, is over 400 years old. The huge room has a paneled ceiling and a wonderful old-fashioned interior. Suspended over the Seine, it offers an exceptional view of the heart of Paris. To the left is the Notre-Dame and the Île de la Cité and to the right is the Île Saint-Louis and the Quai d'Orléans, lined with poplar trees. From the Île Saint-Louis, sister island of the Île de la Cité, with its genuine seventeenth-century setting, one discovers the most beautiful view that can be had of the choir roof of the Notre-Dame.

77. *The Pont des Arts, 1950.* Edouard Boubat.

78. *The Pont des Arts, 1974.* (Ibid.) Dating from the early nineteenth century, this was Paris's first metal bridge. It is only open to pedestrians. The Pont des Arts was completely reconstructed in 1984 after a barge collided with it and destroyed one of its arches. It offers a view of exceptional beauty. These two photographs are perfectly complementary and reveal the full length of the Pont-Neuf in the distance. On the right bank are the two theaters of the Place du Châtelet, the top of the Saint-Jacques tower, and in the background the rooftops of Town Hall. Behind the trees of Vert-Galant, the quai and the bend in the Quai des Orfèvres is the spire of the Sainte-Chapelle. Thanks to the musicians, painters, lovers and strollers who visit this footbridge, it is an ideal promenade and a place of peace and quiet.

79. *The Pont Alexandre-III, 1900.* Robert Demachy—Bichromated gum (La Société française de photographie). This bridge was constructed for the Exhibition of 1900 and named after Czar Alexander III, in celebration of the Franco-Russian alliance. His son, Czar Nicholas II, laid the first stone in 1896.

80. *Steamboats on the Seine, 1945.* Seeberger. One subject, two different views, two different worlds. Demachy, leader of the French pictorialist school, made use of all the resources of parallel techniques to create his work. Working with precious types of paper, more concerned with effect than with subject matter and convinced that "in art it is not the motive, but the way of showing it that's important," Demachy and his friends created a style of spectacular pictures that were not unlike engravings, wash-drawings or charcoal sketches. Ink and bichromated gum can, in the best of cases, produce strangely poetic works. Pictorialism, in keeping with the bourgeois painting of the Belle Epoque, "is to photography what the Modern Style is to architecture" (Y. Christ). Even though this trend did not last in the war between the fuzzy and the sharp image, Pictorialism produced some marvelously evocative photographs. It wasn't long before photography regained the upper hand and offered works like this naturalistic picture in which Seeberger brings to life a powerful reality.

Grey or black smoke, or white like the eyes of the blind, are rising and blurring the landscape, but the small steamboats under my window let out a sudden, odd cry. (Francis Carco, Maman Petit Doiqt.)

81. *Under the Pont des Arts, 1900.* Robert Demachy.

82. *'A Barge in the Night, 1929.* André Kertész.

Photographs 81 and 82 illustrate the conflict between artistic and naturalistic trends. Demachy made use of pigment processes to create a unique picture, very closely resembling a charcoal sketch. In contrast, Kertész, the highly innovative and original photographer "to whom we all owe something" (Cartier-Bresson), respected the very nature of nature and used simple reality to create an effect. The artificial pigment was replaced by the silvery grain:

I love to watch the Seine and its quais from my window on those gray, tender mornings that lend an intimate softness to things (Anatole France, Le Crime de S. Bonnard).

83. *Booksellers on the quai de Montebello, 1956.* Izis. The quais of the Seine, lined with elms, plane trees or poplars, have always attracted a diverse crowd. Of the washing and bathing places that were installed, only the baths of Deligny survive. As far as the booksellers are concerned, they did not obtain the right to have permanent stalls until the end of the nineteenth century.

The Quai de Montebello, running along Viviani Square—another popular spot—is located right next to the oldest church of Paris, Saint-Julien-le-Pauvre, and is across the Seine from the Cathedral of Notre-Dame. From the quai, one has a wonderful view of the gardens of the Archdiocese.

The damp sky, swollen with moisture, gave to the zinc, the slate of the roofs, the sidewalks and even the surface of the water, a moiré sheen of reflections, of grays, of nuances, the range of which, when I call it to mind, almost makes me shudder (Francis Carco, Envoûtement de Paris).

84. *The Barge with the Children, 1959.* Willy Ronis.

85. *Quai de l'Arsenal, 1965.* Izis.

Seen from the Pont d'Arcole (to the left), a train of barges goes up the Seine in the direction of the westernmost edge of the Île Saint-Louis; on the left is the Quai Bourbon and the Pont Louis-Philippe; on the right, the Quai d'Orléans across from the footbridge of Saint-Louis.

86. *The Tree of Vert-Galant, 1961.* André Martin.

87. *Gardens of the Archdiocese, 1983.* Christophe Boisveux.

The famous tree of Vert-Galant and the gardens of the Archdiocese, near the wall with the age-old ivy, are ideal spots for lovers to dream away and murmur soft words in each other's ears.

88. *Quai du Louvre, 1920.* Auguste Léon (Kahn collection).

89. *Quai des Célestins, 1903.* Anonymous (Rapho).

At the beginning of the nineteenth century the port of Paris became more and more important and the capital was one of the first harbor complexes of France. Everywhere in the heart of the city, from the Port of Saint-Bernard (Austerlitz) to the Port des Invalides, there was enormous activity on the water. The boat moored here at the Quai du Louvre was sometimes called "the London," because of its direct and regular service between Paris and London. In the background are the Pont des Arts, la Cité, and the Institute.

The Quai des Célestins was the watering place for dogs and horses. It was also the place where horses were currycombed and where dog trimmers and cat "cutters" exercised their art.

90, 91. *Quai de Seine, ca. 1930.* Man Ray.
One sees the Seine loaded with boats, barges, ferries and long tree trunks carried along by the current. The river used to be the vital route by which food and fuel were brought in; it was also the most convenient, if not the quickest way to travel in an age when travel was a relatively slow-going affair.
(T'Serstevens, La Seine à Paris.)

92. *The Point of Vert-Galant, 1961.* André Martin.

At the head of the Île de la Cité below the Pont-Neuf where there was the statue of Henry IV, the island ended in a point like the sharp bow of a ship and there was a small part at the water's edge with fine chestnut trees, huge and spreading (E. Hemingway, A Moveable Feast).

93. *Quai Malaquais, 1982.* Jean-Claude Gautrand.

94. *Pont de Bercy, 1982.* Philippe Gautrand.

95. *Quai d'Anjou, 1962.* André Martin.

At that spot the violence of the current was such that it looked like a cataclysm that could not be arrested. There (and the same can be said of Bercy) the waves rose higher than the banks—which were partially flooded—and the speed with which they rushed forward was accentuated in the vast stretch opening up before them. One had the impression that not only the surroundings but the whole countryside was going to be ravaged by this whirling cloud of yellowish spray, strewn with butterflies
(F. Carco, Envoûtement de Paris).

96. *Quai de Seine, Passy, 1978.* Claude Raimond-Dityvon.

97. *Point of Vert-Galant, 1948.* Izis.

98. *Quai de Montebello, 1976.* Peter Turnley.

99. *Quai d'Orléans, 1970.* Izis.

I could spend my whole life watching the Seine flow by . . . It is a poem of Paris. (Blaise Cendrars, Paris des rêves.)

100. *The Pont-Neuf, 1861/1862*. Adolphe Braun (Unterlinden Museum, Colmar). This monument of monuments is the most famous bridge of Paris. The first stone was laid in 1578, by Henri III, but the work on the bridge was not completed until 1605. Henri IV was the first to cross it, on horseback. The equestrian statue was erected in 1818. Although the bridge underwent several restorations, the main part of it is the same as it was 350 years ago. Many factors contributed to the Pont-Neuf being a fashionable promenade at the time: the high sidewalks that protected pedestrians from the traffic, the open view of the river and of the beautiful hotels of the Quai Saint-Augustin nearby, the small boutiques in the cut-aways and last, but not least, the many street shows and performances by jugglers, mimes, and other hucksters. The view in the photograph is toward the Rue Dauphine.

101. *The Pont-Neuf, 1971*. Jean Gaumy.
The garden of Vert-Galant is one of the least-known spots of Paris. One enters it via a kind of Mycenaean portico that could serve as a setting for Sophocles's Electra *(T'Serstevens)*.

102. *Autumn Morning on the Quai d'Anjou, 1950*. Albert Monier. The Quai d'Anjou still has its seventeenth-century decor and atmosphere. In the silence of a northern light, modest houses and sumptuous hotels, such as the Hôtel Lambert and the Hôtel Lazun, stand side by side in utter harmony.

103. *At the Vert-Galant, at Night, 1931*. René-Jacques.

104. *Passerelle des Arts, 1934*. Brassaï.
The Seine at night is a dragonfly, artfully pinned by the head to the cork of Paris, with the Notre-Dame as an ornament (Robert Giraud, Le Vin des rues*)*.

105. *Île de la Cité, 1964*. Alain Perceval. Extraordinary aerial view of the Île de la Cité and the Île Saint-Louis, both solidly braced to the banks by some of the thirty-one bridges of Paris. In the foreground is the Pont-Neuf; on the left, the Pont au Change, the Pont Notre-Dame, the Pont d'Arcole, the Pont Louis-Philippe, the Pont Marie; on the right, the Pont Saint-Michel, the Petit-Pont, the Pont au Double, the Pont de l'Archevêché, the Pont de la Tournelle and the Pont Sully. On the right bank are the two theaters of the Place du Châtelet, the tower of Saint-Jacques, Town Hall and the Church of Saint-Gervais. On the island is the statue of Vert-Galant, the foliage of the Place Dauphine, the Palais de Justice, the Sainte-Chapelle, the Hôtel-Dieu, Notre-Dame and the gardens of the Archdiocese.

106. *Chevet of the Notre-Dame, 1852*. Jules Couppier (La Bibliothèque nationale). The restoration works have started, but the cathedral does not yet have the high spire (295 feet) that was added by Viollet-le-Duc in 1860. To the left of the cathedral is the first hospital of the Hôtel-Dieu; it was destroyed in 1854.

107. *The Tar-Sprayer, 1947/1948*. René Jacques.

108, 109. *Interior of Notre-Dame, 1961*. André Martin. The construction of Notre-Dame, funded by Bishop Maurice de Sully, began in 1163 during the reign of Louis VII; the building was not completed until 1330, 170 years after the first stone had been laid. A cross between Roman and Gothic style, Notre-Dame underwent a full-scale restoration in 1841 under the direction of Viollet-le-Duc.
The transept is 157 feet wide; the vault rises 115 feet. The main nave shows eight vaulted bays, two by two (photo 108). The galleries were built over the aisles (photo 109).

110. *The caretaker of Notre-Dame, 1978*. Martine Franck.

111. *Japanese Tourists in Front of Notre-Dame, 1978*. Martine Franck.

112. *Two Friends in the Sun by Notre-Dame, 1977*. Jean-Philippe Charbonnier.

113. *Large Woman in a Loud Check, 1979*. Jean-Philippe Charbonnier.

114. *A Beautiful Spanish Lady, Perhaps a Bit Moorish, 1979*. Jean-Philippe Charbonnier.

115. *From the Top of Notre-Dame, 1952*. Henri Cartier-Bresson.

116. *Little Girl, Quai d'Orléans, 1948/1950*. Daniel Masclet.

117. *The Deportation Memorial, Square of the Île-de-France, ca. 1960*. Daniel Masclet.
Within the memorial building, urns containing the ashes of deportation victims and the grave of the unknown deportee commemorate the suffering of millions of Nazi camp martyrs: "Forgive, but do not forget."

73. Emmanuel Sougez, 1945.

74. Henri Cartier-Bresson, 1961.

75. René-Jacques, 1950.

76. René-Jacques, 1938.

77. Edouard Boubat, 1950.

78. Izis, 1974.

79. Robert Demachy, 1900.
80. Seeberger, 1945.

81. Robert Demachy, 1900.

82. André Kertész, 1929.

83. Izis, 1956.

84. Willy Ronis, 1959.

85. Izis, 1965.

86. André Martin, 1961.

87. Christophe Boisvieux, 1983.

88. Auguste Léon, 1920.

89. Anonyme / Anonymous, 1903.

90. Man Ray, ca. 1930.

91. Man Ray, ca. 1930.

92. André Martin, 1961.

93. Jean-Claude Gautrand, 1982.

94. Philippe Gautrand, 1982.

95. André Martin, 1962.

96. Claude Raimond-Dityvon, 1978.

97. Izis, 1948.

98. Peter Turnley, 1976.

99. Izis, 1970.

100. Adolphe Braun, 1861/1862.

101. Jean Gaumy, 1971.

102. Albert Monier, 1950.

103. René-Jacques, 1931.
104. Brassaï, 1934.

105. Alain Perceval, 1964.

106. Jules Couppier, 1852.

107. René-Jacques, 1947/1948.

108. André Martin, 1961.

109. André Martin, 1961.

110. Martine Franck, 1978.

111. Martine Franck, 1978.

112. Jean-Philippe Charbonnier, 1977.

113. Jean-Philippe Charbonnier, 1979.

114. Jean-Philippe Charbonnier, 1979.

115. Henri Cartier-Bresson, 1952.

116. Daniel Masclet, 1948/1950.

117. Daniel Masclet, ca. 1960. ▶

CHAPTER IV

MONTMARTRE

In New York there is Greenwich Village, in London there is Soho, and in Paris there is Montmartre. It's a good bet that the watering holes of Montmartre have been popular for far longer than those of the other two neighborhoods. Millions of years ago, prehistoric animals came to this hill to quench their thirst along the banks of the Seine; their bones were discovered by Cuvier in the Parisian limestone. On this same hill, the Romans built two temples, one consecrated to Mars, the other to Mercury. It was in front of the latter, on Mount Martyrium, that Saint Denis was beheaded.

A small chapel was established here in the sixth century, and the surrounding area became a nunnery in 1133, the Abbey of the Dames-de-Montmartre, or the Upper Abbey. The Church of Saint-Pierre-de-Montmartre, the oldest surviving church in Paris, was also built in this period. Apparently the nuns sometimes kicked up their heels, and the abbey soon acquired a reputation not entirely in keeping with a pious institution. This notoriety has been traced to a visit there by Henry IV, nicknamed the Gay Old Spark, at the time of the Siege of Paris. In 1692 a priory was built about half way down the hill, on the spot where Saint Denis had been executed, and became known as the Lower Abbey.

At the time of the Revolution, the abbey's goods were confiscated, divided up and sold, mostly to quarries and masons. The buildings were demolished, and new, open limestone quarries were broached: the Montmartre plaster had in fact been prized since antiquity for its hardness and its brilliant whiteness. At the end of the eighteenth century, the butte of Montmartre was a verdant hill graced with numerous mills, planted with vineyards and orchards watered by plentiful springs. The slopes were steep and cloven by deep gorges. At the top of the hill, a church, cemetery, public square (the Place du Tertre), and a few narrow streets made up the hamlet.

Established in 1790, the Municipality of Montmartre flourished after the Revolution, especially during Haussmann's building campaign in the mid-nineteenth century. Expropriation and demolition drove many Parisians away, but it was during this time that many entertainers and artists settled in the district. Yet the face of the hill hardly changed until 1854. In his Promenades et Souvenirs, Gérard de Nerval described this rustic village: "There, there are mills, cabarets and arbors, elysian fields and silent alleys bordered by thickets, cottages, barns and gardens; green plains cut through by precipices where streams filter through the loam, little by little defining certain small islands of green, where goats frolic." Montmartre's rustic character was to remain almost intact until World War I. The sole exception was the construction of the Byzantine-style basilica of the Sacré-Coeur in 1875. By then it had acquired its reputation as "the refuge of artists." Painters, engravers, writers and draughtsmen settled in this cheerfully raucous, bohemian area. Picasso lived there, as did Utrillo, Renoir and Toulouse-Lautrec. Montmartre was home to the cabaret acts of Rictus, Bruant and Fredé, to the surrealist Max Jacob and to the poet Guillaume Apollinaire.

Such fame, unfortunately, has had a negative impact on the area. The influx of flâneurs and sightseers brought about the rapid growth of commerce in the streets and completely transformed the district. Montmartre became a vast movie set with sham painters, sham bistros and sham folklore for naive tourists. Today it is only a gaudy caricature of what it once was. And yet, one can still find, in the calm of the morning, a few old streets full of charm and tenderness, and some hidden, peaceful gardens. But if you wish to know what Montmartre was really like—with its old mills and steep streets and breathtaking views—simply turn the page.

118. *The Mills of Montmartre, 1842.* Hippolyte Bayard—Calotype (La Bibliothèque historique de la Ville de Paris). One of Bayard's most beautiful calotypes (positive direct on paper), unfortunately, only a reproduction has survived, a witness to the period during which the butte of Montmartre was afloat with the sails of windmills.

Numbering thirteen at the beginning of the nineteenth century, the mills were a fashionable attraction and many Parisians sought them out on their Sunday walk. Today, only two still stand; the Blute-Fin and the Moulin de la Galette.

119. *The Butte of Moulins-Montmartre, ca. 1860.* Gustave Le Gray (La Bibliothèque nationale). This rustic picture of a farandole of mills looking down on quarries and brush recalls the provincial character of Montmartre in the mid-1880s. This is one of Gustave Le Gray's best calotypes.

> At first blush the eye sees this mount, [. . .]
> Where of thirty mills the sails
> stretched straight
> Inform me every day which wind it is
> that chases the high clouds
> (Regnard, 17th cent)

120. *Moulin de la Galette, ca. 1840.* Anonymous (La Bibliothèque nationale). The interior mechanism, the stairs and the millstones of the old mill Radet—later renamed *Moulin de la Galette*—have remained intact. After having been moved several times, the mill became a tavern frequented by the working classes. A popular spot for dancing, it soon became famous. Next to it is the *Blute-Fin*.

> Sundays we still climb
> Via the scenic paths
> To the Moulin de la Galette [. . .].
> (Albert Merat, Tableaux parisiens)

121. *Opening of the Rue Tholozé, 1840/1850.* Hippolyte Bayard—Calotype (La Société française de photographie).

122. *Rue du Mont-Cenis, ca. 1920.* Anonymous (Viollet collection). At the top of the Rue du Mont-Cenis, at number 18, was the house of the famous singer Mimi Pinson; number 21 housed Berlioz from 1834 to 1837. Both houses were demolished in 1925.

123. *Festival in Montmartre, ca. 1862.* Adolphe Braun (Unterlinden Museum, Colmar).

> I've read in old books,
> Written by the Parisians,
> That each year on the Feast of St. Pierre's,
> There's a big procession to Montmartre,
> And in a vein of foreign frivolity
> A long festival to the sound of the carillon.
> (Albert Merat, Tableaux parisiens)

124. *Children in Montmartre, ca. 1925.* Anonymous (Viollet collection).

125. *The Painter behind the Moulin de la Galette, 1903/1904.* Seeberger.

126. *Allée des Brouillards, ca. 1898.* Seeberger. On the south side of this short avenue a crazy kind of construction was erected in place of the old cow-house, where the Parisians used to come to buy milk. It was the Château des Brouillards, where Gérard de Nerval lived in 1846.

In 1850, the area where the outbuildings stood was transformed into a number of plots, and the kitchen gardens of the château became the famous *maquis* (bush) of Montmartre. The château itself was broken up and transported to various locations.

127. *Water-Carrier, Rue des Saules, 1898.* Seeberger. In the seventeenth century, this street was only a dirt road running down to the Clignancourt countryside, lined with numerous willows (*saules*)—hence the name. This picture is typical for the village of Montmartre at the end of the nineteenth century, when only a few of the houses were equipped with running water.

128. *On the Balcony, 1906.* Commandant Puyo (La Société française de photographie). This picture exemplifies the work of the pictorialist school. Puyo employed the bichromated ink technique.

129. *In Front of le Lapin Agile, 1958.* Charles Ciccione (Rapho). Located at the corner of the Rue Saint-Vincent and the Rue des Saules, the famous cabaret *Lapin Agile* dates from 1860: In those days it was a tavern with a signboard that read *Au Rendez-Vous des Voleurs*. After the painter André Gill had decorated the front with an amusing picture of a rabbit coming out of a saucepan, people started to call it *Le Lapin Gill,* which then became *le* Lapin Agile.

Among the famous customers were Courteline, Alphonse Allais, Forain, Renoir and Verlaine. Bruant bought it in 1903 and it quickly became the favorite haunt of the bohemians of Montmartre—Max Jacob, Apollinaire, Carco, Dullin, Utrillo, Picasso, Mac Orlan, among others.

Long before the war, they all met at his place, the artists and poets of the Butte. In the company of all the riffraff of the neighborhood, they spent their evenings there, by the light of a lamp covered with a red scarf . . . (Francis Carco).

130. *Place du Tertre, 1982.* Jean-Claude Gautrand. In the sixteenth century, the square bordered the enclosing wall of the abbey of Montmartre. It was here, in 1871, that the National Guard assembled a large number of cannons. When the government attempted to have the battery removed, there was an uprising, resulting in the revolt of the Commune.

Nowadays, the Place du Tertre is very popular with tourists. They go there to have a portrait done or just to see the sights—the numerous painters and sketchers who work there.

131. *Place du Tertre, 1977.* Muñoz de Pablos.

132. *Grape-Harvesting Festivities, 1975.* François Le Diascorn. Another piece of folklore: the festivities accompanying the yearly harvest of the tiny Montmartre vineyard (Rue Saint-Vincent). The harvest is celebrated with great pomp and every year there is an auction sale of a hundred or so bottles.

133. *Place du Tertre, 1952.* Henri Cartier-Bresson.

134. *Sky of Montmartre, 1981.* Jean-Claude Gautrand. The hill and the basilica (constructed between 1875 and 1912), seen from the terrace of the Galeries Lafayette.

135. *Parisian Sky, 1945.* René-Jacques. View of the Institute.

136. *Montmartre, 1903/1904.* Seeberger.

137. *The Moulin de la Galette, 1982.* Jean-Claude Gautrand.

138. *The Widow Montmartre, 1957.* Bruce Davidson. On his 1956 trip to Paris, Bruce Davidson met an old lady in Montmartre, the widow of the Impressionist painter Léon Fauchet, who had worked with Gauguin. He made a photo essay around the widow Montmartre, as he called her, entitled "the Paris of Madame Fauchet."

139. *Little Girl Trundling a Hoop, 1954.* Edouard Boubat.

140. *Small Dog in Montmartre, 1932/1933.* Brassaï.

The shadows of Paris . . . where in the city are they the most beautiful? Those up in Montmartre are beyond compare (Audiberti).

141. *Stairs, 1948.* René-Jacques.

> *They light the lamps along the walls,*
> *And the star and the flames make*
>   *fantastic zigzags.*
>   *(Verlaine, Poems saturniens.)*

142. *Rue Saint-Rustique, ca. 1900/1905.* Robert Demachy.

143. *The Widow Montmartre, 1957.* Bruce Davidson.

144. *Rue de la Bonne, 1950.* René-Jacques.

145. *Boulevard de la Chapelle, 1960.* Jean-Claude Gautrand.

But only at night does the quarter show its true face, and the atmosphere becomes fantastic and sordid . . . when la Chapelle is good, this country of a marvellous balefulness, and taking—this paradise of the caught red-handed—the brats of the bells. . . . The streets are empty, bleak and gloomy. . . . (Léon-Paul Fargue, Le Piéton de Paris)

118. Hippolyte Bayard, 1842.

119. Gusta

ca. 1860.

120. Anonyme / Anonymous, ca. 1840.

121. Hippolyte Bayard, 1840/1850.

122. Anonyme / Anonymous, ca. 1920.

123. Adolphe Braun, ca. 1862.

124. Anonyme / Anonymous, ca. 1925.

125. Seeberger, 1903/1904.

126. Seeberger, ca. 1898.

127. Seeberger, 1898.

128. Commandant Puyo, 1906.

129. Charles Ciccione, 1958.

130. Jean-Claude Gautrand, 1982.

131. Angel Muñoz de Pablos, 1977.

132. François Le Diascorn, 1975.

133. Henri Cartier-Bresson, 1952.

134. Jean-Claude Gautrand, 1981.

135. René-Jacques, 1945.

136. Seeberger, 1903/1904.

137. Jean-Claude Gautrand, 1982.

138. Bruce Davidson, 1957.

139. Edouard Boubat, 1954.

140. Brassaï, 1932/1933.
141. René-Jacques, 1948.

142. Robert Demachy, ca. 1900/1905.

143. Bruce Davidson, 1957. ▶

144. René-Jacques, 1950.

145. Jean-Claude Gautrand, 1960.

CHAPTER V

PARIS PROMENADING

Oh! to stroll in Paris! delightful and delicious existence!
To promenade is a science, gastronomy for the eye.
To walk is to vegetate, to promenade is to live.

—*Balzac, Physiologie du mariage*

Late in the seventeenth century, King Louis XIV decided that the fortified bastions that had protected Paris since the fourteenth century were no longer necessary. Demolished in 1700, they were replaced by a vast, tree-planted esplanade stretching from the Bastille to the Madeleine. The promenade was called "the Boulevard" from the military term given to the terreplein of a rampart. Situated in an open area, it remained unused until the middle of the eighteenth century. Then gentlemen and passers-by began to stroll there and to populate the handsome townhouses, which had belonged to the high dignitaries of the *Ancien Regime*. To the east, between the Bastille and the Porte Saint-Denis, was the liveliest section of the Boulevard, known as the "Boulevard du Crime." There, a permanent fair offered all sorts of attractions: theaters, balls, circuses, cabarets and restaurants.

If the Boulevard du Crime was the playground of Parisian outdoor life, the Boulevard des Italiens to the west, with its more high-toned atmosphere, became the meeting place of the chic and famous. Under the *Directoire*, the gay blades and the *Merveilleuses* in their alluring gowns promenaded ostentatiously. They were succeeded, under Louis XVIII, by the swells who wore large cravats wound around their necks; later, during the reign of Louis Philippe, came the dandies who copied the fashionable London style.

Around 1862, other boulevards became popular. Citizens of the Second Empire crowded the Boulevards Montmartre, des Capucines and la Madeleine where the more fashionable cafés flourished: the Café Anglais, the Bains Chinois, Frascati and above all Tortono, whose prestigious sidewalk was a favored rendezvous for all the celebrities. "At 11:30 at night, you broke your back to eat an ice cream at Tortoni before going to bed. Thousands were consumed on a summer's eve," wrote Musset. One of the more important theaters of the day, the Folies Dramatiques, opened on the Boulevard Saint-Martin close to the new Ambigu Theater (the old one having burned down). Many improvements to the boulevards were made: Gaslights were installed, pavements were covered with asphalt, the bus line Madeleine-Bastille made its appearance and shops overran miles of promenade. As described by one of their chroniclers, Louis Esnault, the boulevards became "—the center of the world—the end of everything, the supreme goal of so much effort, the pinnacle of so much ambition: to appear, to glitter on the asphalt of this sidewalk, to conquer the place where one languished, and there to become notorious. The boulevard accepted everything provided one had fresh gloves, polished boots and a new hat." The magician Robert

Houdini performed there (his surname was later adopted by Harry Houdini), and Georges Méliès showed his cinematographic projections. For a while it was *the place* until Haussmann's transformations accelerated the process of evolution and the elegant strollers were succeeded by a stream of rushing passers-by caught up in essentially commercial preoccupations.

Sadly, the literary cafés, theaters, and handsome townhouses have been replaced today by the aggressively lit confusion of cinemas, run-of-the-mill restaurants and commercial businesses. This applies even to the Left Bank and the Boulevard Saint-Germain, although its many young students still lend an exciting vitality to the district.

The canal Saint-Martin also retains a certain charm, and its embankments provide an agreeable promenade despite the irritating stream of cars. Deserted by barges, the canal remains: It glides under the drawbridge of the Rue de Crimée, where a sign still warns that it is forbidden to gallop across the bridge! It runs alongside abandoned docks, which have now been transformed into artists's ateliers, and ignores the deserted charcoal-burners's quay and the din of the elevated Metro to meander toward the most interesting point of its course—the Quais Jemmapes and Valmy, where its level equals that of the asphalt of neighboring streets. The attraction offered there by the canal, wedged as it is along the length of a square and curtained off by the foaming water cascading from the locks, is a respite from the city's frantic pace. Then the canal ducks under the Boulevard Richard-Lenoir to resurface at the foot of the Bastille, after which it pours into the brand-new marina of Paris. (The ambition of the town councillor is to make this navigable artery one of the major attractions of the eastern part of the city. The warehouses of la Villette are being restored and transformed into cultural centers.) La Villette's basin then narrows past reforested and shaded banks to become a true nautical boulevard. Currently in the initial stages of its development, the canal affords Parisians an astonishing and poetic stretch of countryside. From the Parc de la Villette to the Quai Anatole-France, the barge *le Patache* provides an ideal way to see the canal. Drifting from lock to lock, bridge to bridge and through the arresting underground passage of the Boulevard Richard-Lenoir where every fifty meters ventilation shafts allow columns of sunlight to slant through, this picturesque boat discovers for its passengers the sights and panoramas of a Paris little known to most.

The district of les Halles has experienced a total upheaval of its landscape, and the area has lost most of the vestiges of its charm. Only photographs can revive memories of this once most characterful parts of the city, this "belly of Paris," as Zola put it.

Originally, les Halles was simply a field reclaimed from the ancient swamps. Around A.D. 1100, it was the site of the city's first public market, an immense bazaar where everything was offered for sale: textiles, comestibles and dry goods. Philip Augustus built the first two enclosed buildings, which were called les Halles, around 1200. One was dedicated to the drapers, the other to the weavers. Saint Louis soon added three more buildings: two for the freshly caught fish arriving from northern ports (near the Rue des Poissonniers and the Faubourg-Poissonnière). Philip the Bold later added one market hall for the cobblers. In the ancient market halls, the "market of the king" was open three days a week, during which the king collected taxes on the proceeds of all sales.

In 1553, Henri II had the halls rebuilt and established new buildings surrounded by houses with arcades (the pillars of les Halles), including markets for meat, eggs and cloth. In 1788, a market for vegetables was founded on the site of the Cimetière des Innocents. The district hardly changed until the middle of the nineteenth century. However, its population grew so quickly that at the beginning of the sixteenth century it became necessary to replace the inadequate parochial chapel with Saint-Eustache, the first stone of which was laid by François I. Saint-Eustache, completed in 1637, and Notre-Dame (which partly inspired it) are among the two most beautiful churches in Paris. Gothic in structure with renaissance decorations, Saint-Eustache also houses one of the more beautiful organs to be found in Paris. In this church, Richelieu, Molière, and the Marquise de Pompadour were baptized; Louis XIV made his first communion; Lulli was married; and Molière, La Fontaine, and Mirabeau all had their funerals. The king's pillory was established in les Halles in the time of Saint Louis—the condemned were attached to a horizontal wheel and thus displayed to the public. The pillory was abolished by Louis XVI in 1786.

In 1856 the whole area was disrupted when Baltard tore down the standing structures and built has magnificent ten pavilions of cast iron and glass. For almost a century it was a scene of teeming and colorful crowds where the world of work and the world of recreation mingled.

In 1971, the area from Saint-Eustache to Saint-Merri was razed to the ground. From the ruins of the eighteenth-century houses now rises the steel and concrete of a complex more industrial than architectural, the Forum des Halles (as yet incomplete). Nearby, in front of Saint-Merri, the arrogant steel and glass architecture of the Centre Pompidou asserts itself proudly on its tubular, colorful structure. These two imposing complexes, one commercial and the other cultural, have changed the flavor of the neighborhood as drastically as they have altered the Parisian style. To judge whether the new construction is an improvement or not, one can simply turn the following pages and compare the photographs of before and after.

THE BOULEVARDS

146. *Corner of the Rue de la Paix and the Rue Casanova, 1843*. William Henry Fox Talbot (Science Museum).

147. *Rue de la Paix, 1843*. William Henry Fox Talbot (Science Museum).

Two pictures of two-fold historic significance: They were among the very first photographs ever taken in Paris and, more important, they were the first examples of calotype (the negative-positive process, invented by Talbot) made in Paris. The calotype was a very important invention: Where before there was only one of every photograph, now an unlimited number of prints could be made.

Thanks to the texture of the paper used for the negative, there is something wonderfully granular and warm about photos 146 and 147.

148. *Le Boulevard du Crime, ca. 1855*. Anonymous. Part of the Faubourg du Temple that had existed since the seventeenth century. It was demolished in 1862 and replaced by the Place de la République. Famous for its numerous theaters—the name was attributed to the many popular productions of detective and suspense dramas—the lively boulevard was also very popular for its many cafés, cabarets, restaurants and pastry shops. For nearly three quarters of a century, spectacles and theatricals in all the genres were feted here. The famous Boulevard du Crime got its name from the repertoire produced on these stages where, every evening, Mrs. Man in the Street was induced to weep by abductions, assassinations and poisonings. Les Enfants du paradis, the film by Marcel Carne, recreates to perfection the ambiance of this era and that of the theatrical demimonde which saw the triumph of the actor Frederic Lemaitre and the mime Debureau. Visiting troupes, theaters, celebrated coffee houses like Café Turc and Café d'Apollon competed in their endeavors to titillate the idlers of Paris.

In this photo we see from right to left, the *Théâtre de la Gaité* (formerly the Nicolet Theater), the Imperial Theater (formerly the Olympic Circus) and the Théâtre Historique, founded in 1846 by Alexandre Dumas.

149. *The Army Returns from Italy, August 14, 1850*. Anonymous (Viollet collection). The return from Italy of the victorious troops of the Austrian army was celebrated with a triumphal march through the streets of Paris.

150. *Boulevard Poissonière, ca. 1859/1860*. Anonymous (University of Texas, Austin).

151. *Boulevard Malesherbes at Noon, 1929*. André Kertész.

152. *Place de l'Opéra*. André Kertész.

Five years ago, with the traffic jams getting more and more exasperating, I doubted whether the trams would be able to continue running along the Boulevard de Strasburg, the Boulevard de Sebastopol. A physical impossibility! When the tramways have caused 48 hour traffic jams, they will simply have to decide in favor of getting rid of these hippopotamuses of the traffic. (P. Véron, 1884.)

153. *Snapshot, 1911*. Alfred Stieglitz (Art Institute of Chicago). This snapshot was taken at the beginning of the Boulevard Bonne-Nouvelle by Alfred Stieglitz, the father of modern photography who, in a reaction to the fashionable pictorialism of the period, promoted "pure" photography.

154. *The Effect of the Rain, ca. 1899*. Maurice Bucquet (University of Texas, Austin). The terrace of the famous Café de la Paix, which was decorated by Charles Garnier.

155. *Café de Flore, Early in the Morning, 1976*. Jeanloup Sieff. Once the favorite spot of Apollinaire and Maurras, this famous café later became the "headquarters" of the existentialists.

156. *Café Terrace, Boulevard Saint-Germain, 1969*. Izis.

> *At Saint-Germain-des-Pres my loves they died*
> *And my mute lips cling to lips*
> *And steal kisses like a beggar steals bread*
> *While in me dies the fire of my youth.*
> *(Mouloudji)*

THE CANAL

157. *Canal Saint-Martin, 1971*. Angel Muñoz de Pablos. The footbridges over the canal seen from the intersection of the Rue de Lancry and the Quai de Jemmapes.

At certain times, the canal . . . with its locks, its footbridges with gardens and its tranquil water evokes an unforgettable atmosphere (Francis Carco, Envoûtement de Paris).

158. *Canal Saint-Martin, 1954*. Izis. The Quai de Valmy where it crosses the Rue de Lancry.

The scene is just a few steps from the Hôtel du Nord, made famous by Marcel Carné's film of the same name.

159. *Canal Saint-Martin, Quai de Valmy, 1976.* Philippe Salaün.

160. *Canal Saint-Martin, Quai de Valmy, 1953.* Robert Doisneau. This canal has no fewer than nine locks and fourteen bridges and footbridges between the basin of la Villette and the Pont d'Austerlitz.

161. *Model, 1978.* Elliot Erwitt.

162. *The Lock-Keeper, 1955.* Edouard Boubat. The lock at the corner of the Quai de Valmy and the Rue du Faubourg-du-Temple.

163. *The Basin of la Villette, 1963.* Jean-Philippe Charbonnier. The warehouses of the Quai de Seine—now renovated to provide lofts for artists—and the wheels of the drawbridge of Crimée.

> *Two docks, tall and brown, stand one*
> *facing the other,*
> *Visibly disjointed by the violence,*
> *And the water between them runs*
> *from their rupture.*
> *(Jules Romains, le Voyage des amants.)*

164. *Quai de Jemmapes, 1938.* René-Jacques. A peaceful scene at the Quai de Jemmapes, near the footbridge of the Rue Léon-Jouhaux.

[. . .] if the Canal de l'Ourcq, which yawns, stretches itself and goes back to sleep like a fish-pond between the Quai de la Marne and the Quai de l'Oise, does not succeed in rendering the traveller poetic, it's because he is too particular to make do with a landscape that smacks half of Holland, half of the Rhine. For me, this canal is the Versailles and the Marseille of this proud and stark land. Art risks nothing here; and besides, all the students of Marquet and Utrillo would choose to live here, if they could. (Leon-Paul Fargue, le Pleton de Paris.)

LES HALLES

165. *The Old Market, ca. 1852.* Anonymous (Heftler collection). The market of the Rue des Prouvaires has been in operation since 1818. In front of Saint-Eustache, wooden coverings protect a meat market. Surrounding it are a great number of small soup merchants, cafés and storage areas for handcarts.

166. *The Market at the Square des Innocents, before 1855.* Charles Marville (La Bibliothèque historique de la Ville de Paris). This used to be a very busy fruit and vegetable market. Vendors set up inside the gallery, around the fountain and on the square itself.

> *Were there ever criers to match*
> *these criers?*
> *[. . .]*
> *Everybody talks, no-one answers.*
> *You understand not a thing,*
> *you're all confused,*
> *Everything goes, everything*
> *twists and turns.*
> *(Claude la Petit, Chronique scandaleuse*
> *ou Paris ridicule, 1655.)*

167. *Construction of the Baltard Market, ca. 1868.* Dontenville (La Bibliothèque nationale). Napoléon III detested the massive stone building built by Baltard in 1851 and decided to replace it by "iron umbrellas." Baltard had the building demolished and on the same spot erected his ten famous pavilions. Two more pavilions were built in 1936, east of the Rue Baltard.

168. *Rue de la Tonnellerie, ca. 1855.* Charles Marville (La Bibliothèque historique de la Ville de Paris). In 1866, after the transformation of the quarter, this street was renamed Rue Baltard. Since part of the Rue du Pont-Neuf ran above it, the houses on the left side had arches: "the pillars of Les Halles."

169. *Rue Baltard, 1898.* Anonymous (La Bibliothèque nationale).

With their prodigious masting, les Halles pile up mass on mass geometrically, squarely, uniformly, like some modern machine, a boiler made for the digestive processes of a whole people, a giant metal belly, bolted, rivetted, made of wood, glass, castings. (Emile Zola, le Ventre de Paris)

170. *The Carreau of Les Halles, before 1914.* Seeberger (La Caisse nationale des monuments historiques). "Carreau" is the name for the center location of Les Halles, where vegetables and fruit are sold. Here, vegetable merchants ply their trade in front of Saint-Eustache.

171. *Rue Rambuteau, Last Sales before the Sounding of the Bell, ca. 1897.* Anonymous (Personal collection). Market gardeners and vegetable growers stopped selling at 7:00 P.M. (in the winter at 8:00) with the sounding of the bell.

172. *Vender, 1905/1906*. Louis Vert (La Société française de photographie).

173. *Rue Rambuteau, 1895/1896*. Anonymous (Personal collection).

174. *The Carreau of Les Halles, 1945*. Willy Ronis.

On the other side, at the crossroads of Sainte Eustache, the entry to rue Rambuteau was blocked by a barricade of pumpkins in two lines, sprawling, bloating their orange paunches. (Emile Zola, le Ventre de Paris)

175. *Vendor with Tattooed Arms, 1952*. Henri Cartier-Bresson.

176. *Vegetable Vender, 1929*. André Kertész.

177. *The Carreau of Les Halles, 1953*. Robert Doisneau.

He made his companion admire the day breaking on the vegetables. It was a sea. It extended from the tip of Saint-Eustache to the rue des Halles, between the two groups of pavillions. And at both ends, at the two crossroads, the flood-tide grew even larger, with vegetables inundating the sidewalk. (Emile Zola, le Ventre de Paris)

178. *The Carreau of Les Halles, 1945*. Robert Doisneau.

They passed them from hand to hand, the baskets of early vegetables which the market-gardeners, standing near the harness, were seeing to, stacking them in imposing heaps, even on the road. [. . .] And as the carts, relieved of their burdens of cauliflowers, leeks, carrots and lettuce, were turned around, others took their places in the midst of a concert of abuse, orders, whinnying and smacks of the whip. (Francis Carco, Envoutement de Paris)

179. *Last Snow on Baltard, 1971*. Jean-Claude Gautrand. The last winter before the pavilions of Baltard were demolished.

One December evening, on opening his windows, he found them all white with snow, a virgin whiteness illumining the rust colored sky; [. . .] they had a good silence, the softness of an innocent giant. (Emile Zola, le Ventre de Paris)

180. *The Fall of a Roof, 1971*. Jean-Claude Gautrand.

181. *After the Fall, 1971*. Jean-Claude Gautrand.

> *Blinding, the iron puts out the eye*
> *of the haze*
> *The iron is one immense sore*
> *In the troubled mortal dust*
> *Of strange phantasms*
> *There is some evil in this Paris morning.*
> *(Andre Laude)*

182. *In the Storage Yard of Les Halles, 1979*. Claude Raimond-Dityvon.

183. *The Forum of Les Halles, 1981*. Jean-Claude Gautrand.
In front of Saint-Eustache, the sumptuous 17th century parish church, the "Halles hole" has given birth to a new quarter, for the most part underground. On the lower levels, new roads link Paris with the Ile de France; above them the walkways, lit by arc-lamps and stained glass windows, and lined with all kinds of entertainment, including fashion boutiques, hobby stores, cinemas and restaurants, represent an attempt to recreate in this, the center of Paris, a new, stylish place for flaneurs.

POMPIDOU CENTER

184. *The Centre Pompidou, 1977*. Marc Riboud. View from the Tour Saint-Jacques. In front, the Church of Saint-Merri (sixteenth century). The *Centre national d'art et de culture Georges Pompidou*, located on the Beaubourg plateau, was opened in 1976. It houses not only a museum for modern art but also an acoustic research center (IRCAM) and an enormous library.

185. *View from the Interior of the Pompidou Center, 1981*. Jeanloup Sieff.

186. *The Escalator, 1981*. Philippe Gautrand. The modern shape of the escalator contrasts with the renovated façades of the old houses on the Rue Saint-Martin.

187. *From the Top of Centre Pompidou, 1981.*
Jean-Claude Gautrand. Glass covered corridors
offer spectacular views of Paris from 138 feet
above the ground.
There is a magnificent view from these 42-
meter-high windows in their long corridors:
Paris and the piazza opposite the Centre's main
entrance, a place to meet caricaturists, musicians, acrobats, fire-eaters and all the other
street folk. At the rear, the rue Aubry-le-
Boucher leading to the Forum des halles.

188. *Centre Pompidou, 1976.* Martine Franck.
Part of the external tubing system, seen from
the roof of the Centre Pompidou. In the background is Montmartre.

189. *Ventilation Shafts of the Centre Pompidou,
1981.* Philippe Gautrand.

190. *Couple, 1981.* Willy Ronis.

146, 147. William Henry Fox Talbot, 1843.

148. Anonyme / Anonymous, ca. 1855.

149. Anonyme / Anonymous, ca. 1859.

150. Anonyme / Anonymous, 1859/1860.

151. André Kertész, 1929.

152. André Kertész, 1929.

153. Alfred Stieglitz, 1911.

154. Maurice Bucquet, ca. 1899.

155. Jeanloup Sieff, 1976.

156. Izis, 1969.

157. Angel Muñoz de Pablos, 1971.

158. Izis, 1954.

159. Philippe Salaün, 1976.

160. Robert Doisneau, 1953.

161. Elliott Erwitt, 1978.

162. Edouard Boubat, 1955.

163. Jean-Philippe Charbonnier, 1963.

165. Anonyme / Anonymous, ca. 1852.

166. Charles Marville, ca. 1854.

167. Dontenville, ca. 1868.

168. Charles Marville, ca. 1855.

169. Anonyme / Anonymous, 1898.

170. Seeberger, avant 1914.

171. Anonyme / Anonymous, ca. 1897.

172. Louis Vert, 1905/1906.

173. Anonyme / Anonymous, 1895/1896.

174. Willy Ronis, 1945.

175. Henri Cartier-Bresson, 1952.

176. André Kertész, 1929.

177. Robert Doisneau, 1953.
178. Robert Doisneau, 1945.

179. Jean-Claude Gautrand, 1971.

180. Jean-Claude Gautrand, 1971.

181. Jean-Claude Gautrand, 1971. ▶

182. Claude Raimond-Dityvon, 1979.

mbine Nature

acticality...

fully

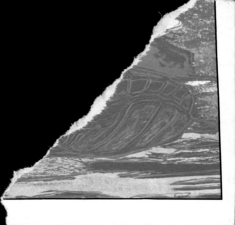

183. Jean-Claude Gautrand, 1981.

184. Marc Riboud, 1977.

185. Jeanloup Sieff, 1981.

186. Philippe Gautrand, 1981.

187. Jean-Claude Gautrand, 1981.

188. Martine Franck, 1976.

189. Philippe Gautrand, 1981.

190. Willy Ronis, 1981.

CHAPTER VI

A BIRD'S EYE VIEW OF PARIS

Stop for a minute and look at the city rising up over the skyline. Regard it carefully. This Paris is also in perpetual motion and offers a host of discoveries and astonishing panoramas. There are many "high points" in Paris, whether they are natural like the mountain of Saint-Geneviève, the butte of Montmartre or the plateau of Belleville, or artificial like the towers of steel and concrete, which more and more elbow each other for attention on the crowded skyline.

The darling of the Parisian horizon, however, continues to be the hundred-year-old Eiffel Tower. A triple challenge to gravity, to opinion and to the functional, this symbol of the industrial era almost wasn't built. When first proposed, the Eiffel Tower provoked a storm of protest. First came the famous "petition des cents" (petition of hundreds) signed by such notable men in the arts and literature as de Maupassant, Dumas, Leconte de Lisle, Meissonier, Gounod, Coppée and Verlaine. They protested "with all their might against the building, right in the middle of the capital, of the useless and monstrous Eiffel Tower," this "skeleton of a belfry" (Verlaine), this "glory of wire and plates—this hideous pillar of grills—[this] tube of factory construction" (Huysmans). To this criticism Eiffel replied: "I believe the tower has its own proper beauty—furthermore, the colossal has something attractive, an inherent charm to which ordinary theories of art hardly apply." Perhaps we would agree with him today.

Constructed on the Champ-de-Mars on the occasion of the Paris Exposition of 1889, the Eiffel Tower was executed with remarkable precision: Three hundred agile construction workers assembled this lacework of steel connected by two and a half million rivets in just eighteen months. In 1919 it was used by the army for relaying long-wave transmissions, and was the site of the first attempts at radio broadcasting in 1921 and then television broadcasting in 1925. In 1983 it celebrated its hundred millionth visitor! Almost a thousand feet high, it was for a long time the tallest building in the world. The view from its summit, which in good weather extends for approximately thirty miles, is extraordinary: Paris whirls around it in a breathtaking panoramic waltz.

To the northeast of the capital, the plateau of Belleville-Ménilmontant rises gently, bordered on the north by the Buttes-Chaumont and on the south by the magnificent foliage of the Père-Lachaise Cemetery.

The old village of Belleville, inhabited by artisans, gardeners, and vine-growers, spills over onto this plateau which could be descended via a rather steep path. At the bottom were foodstands and taverns in which wine flowed freely even on Sunday. For a long time Belleville remained a sleepy urban village. Narrow footpaths wound around the "mountain" between the courtyards and the gardens. In good weather the smells of leather, wood and varnish filled the air, giving way in the evening to the sensuous perfume of wisteria and lilac. Although not exceedingly picturesque, Belleville-Ménilmontant enjoyed the attentions of the photographer Willy Ronis, who excelled in discovering beauty in the images of daily life in this quiet Parisian district. His photographs provide poignant testimony to the people, footpaths, courtyards, houses and inns of a time gone by.

Take a last look at the city's sea of roofs as they flow rhythmically toward the horizon—poetic, surreal, romantic, different from one area to the next, one period to another. Today, imposing terraces of modern buildings contend with colorful, old-fashioned roofs made of tile and zinc, from whose ubiquitous chimneys rise, here and there, a few pale wisps of smoke. "I adore these chimneys," wrote de Vigny. "The smoke of Paris is more lovely to me than the solitude of the woods and mountains."

Although the skyline continues to change rapidly, the roofs of Paris, with their chimneys puffing serenely above the city, remain as enchanting a spectacle as any the capital has to offer.

THE EIFFEL TOWER

191. *Bust of Gustave Eiffel, 1933*. Henry Lacheroy (Octant gallery, Paris). Gustave Eiffel gained his reputation as a bridge builder (the Gabarit Viaduct, among others). He began constructing his famous tower for the occasion of the 1899 World Exposition. Almost 1,000 feet tall, the tower became a symbol of the industrial age. Many notable Parisians objected to its intrusive presence on the city's skyline.

192. *The Construction of the Tower, 1887/1889*. Anonymous (Giraudon/Carnavalet). This photo essay by an unknown photographer was taken at regular intervals, always from the same point of view, over a period of twenty-six months. Altogether, 7,300 tons of iron, 12,000 metal parts and 2,000,000 rivets were required to construct the Tower, which scored an unprecedented success at the Universal Exhibition of 1889. Two million visitors ascended this "gigantic and so original specimen of modern construction methods." (Thomas Edison)

[. . .] The sensation of a building which has gone to sea; but there was not the slightest feeling of seasickness. Once you were up there, a conception, well beyond the thought of any earthly race, of the grandeur, the size, the Babylonian immensity of Paris [. . .] (The Goncourts' Diary, 1889)

193. *The Gardens around the Tower, 1945*. Lucien Hervé. The view from the second platform, 380 feet up in the air.

194. *The Painter of the Eiffel Tower, 1954*. Marc Riboud.
Here, reproduced in iron, the rope which drew the fakir to the skies, the one he invited his friends to climb. (Giraudoux, Priere sur la tour Eiffel)

195. *The Shadow of the Tower, 1937*. François Kollar. The technology and photography pavilion of the 1937 World Exposition in the shadow of the Eiffel Tower.

196. *Shadow of the Tower, 1929*. André Kertész.

197. *The Tower Seen from Sightseeing Boat, 1980*. Lionel Fourneaux.

198. *Couples, 1956*. Charles Harbutt.

199. *Métro Bir-Hakeim, 1973*. Charles Harbutt.

200. *The Tower and the House of the Radio, 1962*. André Martin.
Finished in 1963, the Paris Broadcasting House, on the Quai de Passy, consists of a circular building 175 meters in diameter surmounted by a 65 meter tower, which they say is sinking 3 centimeters per year.

> *Paris raises its tower*
> *just as does a big anxious giraffe*
> *its tower—*
> *who, at evening,*
> *afraid of the phantoms,*
> *goes walking all over the place*
> *with the jets of its projectors.*
>
> *l'Inflation sentimentale.)*
> (Pierre Mac Orlan,

201. *The Champs-Elysées, 1959*. Willy Ronis. The Champ-Elysées and the Arc de Triomphe seen from the terrace of the Tuileries. In the foreground, a detail of the Obélisque with hieroglyphics.

I live between two rivers known all over the world, one green, of water, the other black, of asphalt: the Seine and the Champs-Elysees. (R. Dorgelès, Regards sur Paris)

202. *Place de la Concorde, 1961*. André Martin. Created in honor of Louis XV, the square was named Place de la Révolution in 1792 and Place de la Concorde in 1795. It was here that the royal couple, Louis XV and Marie-Antoinette, among others, were guillotined in 1793. Thirty-three centuries old, the Obelisque, erected in 1836, comes from the temple at Luxor.

203. *Rue de Rivoli, 1962*. André Martin.

204. *Place de la Bastille, 1957*. Willy Ronis. The Place de la Bastille, built in 1792 on the site of the water-trenches of the Bastille, took its present shape only with the tunnelling of the rue de Lyon and the boulevard Henri-IV.
   This huge site, scene of the famous capture of the fortress in 1789, is dominated nowadays by the column of July, erected to the memory of the Parisians killed at the time of the insurrection of the 27th, 28th and 29th of July 1830, better known under the name of the Trois Glorieuses. The spirit of Liberty at the top of the column is 52 meters above ground level.

BELLEVILLE

205. *The Church of Ménilmontant, 1946.*
René-Jacques. The village of Belleville, situated
on a plateau, dates from the eleventh century.
In 1789 it was given independence as a community, but in 1860 this independence was
taken away. At the foot of the hill, there were
factories and quarries. One of these quarries
was used to create the Butte-Chaumont parks.
The rural village of Ménilmontant was the place
where Parisians liked to go for a walk. The village church, Notre-Dame-de-la-Croix, was built
in 1869.

206. *Belleville, 1969.* Henri Cartier-Bresson.

207. *Rue Vilin, 1959.* Willy Ronis. No one
paid more homage to this working-class area
than Willy Ronis. Thanks to his images we can
still sense the village atmosphere and witness
its daily activities.

208. *Courtyard, Rue Piat, 1948.* Willy Ronis.
The Rue Piat, once an access road to the mills,
offers a beautiful view of the city of Paris.

*Let us climb the rue de Belleville to start with.
Turn right at number 50, onto rue Piat. A nice
morning stroll to the Envierges. At the foot of the
steps, rue Vilin with its touch of the peace of the
countryside. A glass of modest white wine
straight from the barrel is about the only unfore-
seen contingency that may arise. At eyelevel, the
Gare de Lyon—if the weather is good, you can
tell the time by the station clock—the Arc de
Triomph and the Eiffel Tower. In a word: from
up here you can see Paris as from nowhere else.
(Clément Lépidis,* le Mal de Paris)

209. *Café des Cascades, 1948.* Willy Ronis.

*At Belleville, friendship is bronze, seldom alu-
minum. At the bistro where we used to meet up,
it was the hard-boiled types, the slightly salted
cream cheeses, the whipper-snappers, the strap-
ping lads that cut a dash. (Clément Lépidis,* le
Mal de Paris)

210. *Rue des Cascades, 1948.* Willy Ronis.
Formerly Musardes path, the street was renamed Rue des Cascades after the waterfalls
that were created to channel Ménilmontant's
rainwater to the drain at Saint-Martin.

211. *Rue Vilin, 1948.* Willy Ronis.

THE ROOFS OF PARIS

212. *Roofs, 1928.* Maurice Tabard.

213. *Parisian Roofs, 1917.* Alvin Langdon
Coburn (George Eastman-House).
*In the daytime, Paris [. . .] spreads out under a
bluish scale of roofing which harmonizes, thanks
to the varied subtlety of two hundred types of
chimneys, with the faintly tinted skies. (Audiberti)*

214. *The Roofs and the Sacré-Coeur Seen from
the Mosque of Paris, 1929.* André Kertész.
*[. . .] which makes you think of certain poor
parts of Paris in the mornings, with their tall,
funnel-shaped chimneys to which the sun lends
the most vivid pinks, the brightest reds; it's quite
a garden, in flower above the houses, flowering
in such varied hues that you would say this was
the horticultural retreat, planted above the city,
of a tulip lover from Delft or Haarlem. (Marcel
Proust,* A la recherche du temps perdu)

215. *Hôtel Claridge, 1948.* Willy Ronis.

216. *Quartier Latin, 1926.* André Kertész.

217. *The Painter.* Van der Elksen. In the background is the Circus Médrano, which no longer
exists.

218. *The Church of Sainte-Anne-de-la-Maison-
Blanche, Rue de Tolbiac, 1976.* Keiichi Tahara
(from the series "Windows").

191. Henri Lacheroy, 1933.

192. Anonyme / Anonymous, 1887, 88, 89.

193. Lucien Hervé, 1945.

194. Marc Riboud, 1954.

195. François Kollar, 1937.

196. André Kertész, 1929.

197. Lionel Fourneaux, 1980.

198. Charles Harbutt, 1956.

199. Charles Harbutt, 1973.

200. André Martin, 1962.

201. Willy Ronis, 1959.

202. André Martin, 1961.

203. André Martin, 1962.

204. Willy Ronis, 1957.

205. René-Jacques, 1946.

206. Henri Cartier-Bresson, 1969.

207. Willy Ronis, 1959.

208, 209. Willy Ronis, 1948.

210. Willy Ronis, 1948.

211. Willy Ronis, 1948.

12. Maurice Tabard, 1928.

213. Alvin Langdon Coburn, 1917.

214. André Kertész, 1929.

215. Willy Ronis, 1948.

216. André Kertész, 1926.

217. Van der Elsken. ▶

218. Keiichi Tahara, 1976.

BIOGRAPHIES AND BIBLIOGRAPHIES

ATGET Jean-Eugène Auguste (1857–1927)
Born in Libourne, Atget was raised in Bordeaux by his grandparents, where upon completion of his schooling it was natural enough that he tried his hand as a sailor. In 1878 he was living in Paris, where he vainly tried to gain entrance to the Conservatoire national de musique et d'art dramatique. Once finished with his military service he returned to Paris, in 1882 (rue des Beaux-Arts) and became an actor in a small theater group, frequented artistic circles, and painted. In 1886 he met Valentine Compagnon, and over a decade later, in 1898, moved to the rue de la Pieté and decided to become a professional photographer. He began taking pictures of street scenes of the old districts and of the small trades in Paris, some of which were printed as postcards by the publisher Porcher. He moved to the rue Campagne-Première near Montparnasse in 1899 and in 1901 made a series portraying the environs of Paris and "art" in old Paris. Around 1907 Atget photographed the center of the capital for the Bibliothèque historique de la Ville de Paris, and in 1910 sold albums which he himself had put together to the Musée Carnavalet and the Bibliothèque national. In 1920 he sold a group of 2,621 negatives of scenes of Paris, which are now kept in the Archives photographiques de la direction du patrimoine. He also made photographs of prostitutes for the painter Dignimont in 1921. He died in 1927, just one year after Valentine Compagnon. Shortly after his death, Berenice Abbott purchased a number of Atget's plates which she displayed and popularized several years later by means of conferences and exhibitions. She lent prints to the exhibition *Film und Foto* (1929) and published *Atget photographe de Paris* in 1930. Her collection is now part of the Museum of Modern Art in New York. Atget's vision and oeuvre have inspired a number of books: *Paris du temps perdu*, with photographs by Atget and text by Proust (Lausanne Edita, 1963); *Atget, magicien du vieux Paris en son époque* (Jean Leroy, 1975); *Eugène Atget, Voyage en ville* (Gassmann-Martinez. Chêne, 1979); there are also four magnificent works made by John Szarkowski for the Museum of Modern Art in New York.

BALDUS Edouard Denis (1813–1882)
Born in Westphalia, the painter Baldus settled in France and exhibited his works in the Salons of 1842, 1847, 1848 and 1851. In 1851 he received one of the commissions of the Mission Héliographique and from that moment turned his energies to photography, specializing in architecture. Between 1853 and 1854 he created an important series of the landscape of the Dauphine and Auvergne which met with success when shown at the Universal Exhibition of 1855. Baldus received various commissions, including photographing the construction of the railroad from Paris to Boulogne, the floodings of the Rhône and the construction of the new Louvre. Around 1860 he once again made photographs of the principal monuments of Paris. Because of his mastery of framing and composition, as well as his personal vision of his subjects, he became one of the outstanding figures in 19th century photography. He published the book entitled *Monuments principaux de la France* (1875).

BAYARD Hippolyte (1801–1887)
Bayard was born in Breteuil-sur-Noye (Oise). His father was a Justice of the Peace. He pursued studies which led him to become first a clerk and then a civil servant in the Ministry of Finance. Bayard attended the gatherings organized by Amaury Duval, where he met the artists of his time and enjoyed an intellectual milieu excited by the discoveries of Daguerre. He tried to capture the image of the darkroom and showed his first *photogénés*—drawings on sensitized paper—on February 5, 1839. On March 20 he succeeded in making positive images. Bayard continued his experiments and on June 24 showed the world for the first time photographs on paper as part of a paintings exhibition. On November 2, the Académie des beaux-arts acknowledged the superiority of Bayard's technique, and several days later he submitted a report to the Académie des sciences. In the 1850s he belonged to the fabulous school of French calotypists and produced lovely images of Paris, particularly of the mills of Montmartre. Bayard founded the Société héliographique in 1851 which later became the Société française de photographie. He was commissioned by the Mission Héliographique to make a series of photographs of Normandy. In association with Bertall, Bayard opened a portrait studio in Paris on the rue de la Madeleine. One of the masters of the calotype process, he was skilled at manipulating light and mass to create landscapes or still lives of an almost modern conception.

BERTSCH Auguste (?–1871)
Bertsch was a founding member of the Société française de photographie. He was an engineer of his craft and his work on micrography, enlarging processes and short exposures gained him an audience. Bertsch opened a studio with Camille d'Arnaud (also known as Nadar) and exhibited his work in the Universal Exhibitions of 1855 and 1857.

BLANQUARD-EVRARD Louis-Désiré (1802–1872)
Blanquard-Evrard was born in Lille. He became a member of the Société héliographique and was a founding member of the Société française de photographie. He perfected and popularized Fox Talbot's calotype process. In 1851 he started a printing studio in Loos-les-Lilles, the first "photographic printing shop." This firm produced a number of photo albums illustrated with calotypes of the greatest French masters. The factory near Lille, which was a precursor of the photomechanical era in photography, closed its doors in 1855. Blanquard-Evrard also published numerous treatises on photography and photographic processes.

BONOLDI
No documentation on this photographer is available.

BOISVIEUX Christophe (1960)
Boisvieux was born in Chatou (Yvelines). After receiving a degree in Economics, he began photographing in 1978. He worked for the Top agency, which he left, however, in 1981. Various figures who influenced him include: Barbey, Doisneau, Roboud, Martine Franck, and Koudelka. Boisvieux traveled to Ireland (1980–81), Istanbul (1982), and Korea (1984). Publications: *Almanach de la photo* (1983), *Photo Magazine* (1983). He exhibited at the Salon de la Photo in October 1983. In 1984 he was awarded the Prix Air France-Ville de Paris.

BOUBAT Edouard (1923)
Born in Paris, Boubat became a free-lance reporter. In 1946 he produced his first photograph entitled: "Little Girl with dead leaves." He exhibited his work for the first time in 1951 along with

Brassaï, Doisneau, Fachetti and Izis. That same year witnessed the start of his collaboration with *Réalités*. Since then he has made photo essays and has had exhibitions all over the world. Among his numerous publications are: *Femmes* (Chêne, 1979), *Miroirs-Autoportraits* (Denoël, 1973), and *La Survivance* (Mercure de France, 1976), which received the Grand Prix du Livre in Arles in 1977. He was awarded the Grand Prix National des Arts for photography in 1985. The simplicity, poetry, rich humanity, and timelessness of his images inspired Jacques Prévert to say: "Boubat is a correspondent of peace."

BRASSAÏ (1899–1984)
Born in Brassó (Transylvania), Brassaï's real name was Gyula Halász. He studied at the Académie des beaux-arts in Budapest, and later Berlin. He began work as a journalist in Paris in 1923, and was to discover photography in Montparnasse. In 1933 he published *Paris la nuit*. Brassaï's was a universal talent: his drawings were admired by Picasso; his sculptures and tapestries were widely exhibited; his gifts as a writer allowed him to pen extraordinary volumes of memoirs such as: *Histoire de Marie* (1948); *Henri Miller grandeur nature* (1975); *Conversation avec Picasso* (1964); *Paris secret des années trente* (1976). His last work, *Artiste de ma vie* (1982), was awarded the Grand Prix de la Litérature given by the Société de gens de lettres. To these books, which were of course illustrated with photographs, must be added the historic work *Graffiti* (1960). Having become a Chevalier des Arts et Lettres in 1974, and received the Légion d'Honneur in 1976, Brassaï was awarded the Grand Prix National des Arts for photography in 1979. He was endowed with an extraordinary sense of observation, incredible creativity and inexhaustible imagination. His photographs, through their spirit of generosity and tenderness, transformed the humblest scenes of daily life into the most fantastic of visions. He knew how to portray authenticity with simplicity. His photographs have been shown virtually worldwide.

BRAUN Adolphe (1812–1877)
Braun was born in Besançon. He created designs for fabrics in Paris, later becoming director of the drawing studio of a spinning mill in Mulhouse. He discovered that photography allowed the precise recording of the floral motifs designed for printed fabrics. In 1848 he opened an industrial enterprise in Dornach which quickly gained worldwide fame for its reproductions of works of art from the principal museums in Europe. His photographs of flowers were exhibited in the Universal Exhibition of 1855. With the Bisson brothers he was one of the first to make photographs high in the mountains. Becoming official photographer to the court of Napoleon III, he made numerous portraits of eminent figures in the Second Empire. A member of the Société française de photographie, he made several photographs and stereoscopic views of Paris, and participated in numerous exhibitions. *Alsace photographie* (1854) is the only complete album remaining from his prolific production (app. 8,000 photographs).

BUCQUET Maurice (1860–1921)
Bucquet was born in Paris. He belonged to Parisian high society and became a member of the Société française de photographie in 1888. He was elected president of the Photo-club de Paris in 1891, at the time a modest association of amateurs which he was to transform into one of the beacons of French photography at the turn of the century. He was made a Chevalier of the Légion d'Honneur in 1900 for his artistic contribution, and was elected vice-president of the Union nationale des Sociétés photographiques de France. Under the auspices of the Photo-club de Paris, he organized numerous national and international exhibitions. He collaborated in the *Revue de la photographie* and published many technical works, including *l'Esthétique photographique*.

CARTIER-BRESSON Henri (1908)
Cartier-Bresson was born in Chanteloup. He studied painting with André Lhote and was acquainted with the Surrealists. He made his first photograph in 1931 and from that time onward traveled the world constantly. He became assistant to Renoir and Becker (1936) and produced several short films, including *Le Retour* in 1944. In 1947 he founded the cooperative agency Magnum with Robert Capa, David Seymour "Chim" and George Rodger. His work has been internationally exhibited in prominent museums and he has published many books, among them: *Images à la sauvette* (1952), *Les Européens* (1955), *Moscou (1955)*, *Flagrants délits* (1968), *Vive la France* (1970), and *Henri Cartier-Bresson photographe* (Delpire, 1980). He devoted his work increasingly to design. The images of Cartier-Bresson, the most classical of the great photographers, illustrate harmony between form and depth, as well as precision and perfection. With his instinct for the decisive moment and composition, Henri Cartier-Bresson has left an indelible imprint on all of photo-journalism.

CHARBONNIER Jean-Philippe (1921)
Charbonnier was born in Paris to a painter father and a mother who was a writer. He made his first appearance in 1939 with cinema portraitist Sam Lévin, and then worked at the Blanc and Demilly Laboratories in Lyon in 1941. In 1944 he began work as a type setter for *Libération*, moving on to *France Dimanche* and in 1955 to *Temps de Paris*. At the end of 1949 he was a stringer for *Point de vue*, with Albert Plécy. In 1950 he joined the staff of the monthly *Réalités* for which he was to make reports from around the world. He also made prestigious albums for OMS, Régie Renault, Carrefour. He began teaching at the Ecole Supérieure des Arts Graphiques in Paris in 1976. He has had numerous exhibitions in France (Musée d'Art Moderne de Paris in 1983) and abroad: Stockholm, Lausanne, Chicago. His publications include: *Les Chemins de la vie* (1975), and *Un photographe vous parle* (Grasset, 1961). A vision directly engaged with reality, an alert sensitivity, and a good measure of humor have allowed him to photograph the humblest as well as the most favored human beings in all corners of the world, and to record moments full of tenderness for both adults and children. He presently takes many photographs of Paris, where "the exotic is just around the corner from one."

CICCIONE Charles (1912)
Ciccione was born in Marseilles and pursued technical studies from 1924 to 1928. He worked as a draftsman with the firm of Rateau in 1929 and 1930, and later with SUME. He followed night courses at the Ecole Estienne and the Conservatoire National des Arts et Métiers, and worked as a draftsman and photographer for various projects until the war. From 1940 to 1953 he was the head of the photography lab at the SNCF, later becoming a photographer for the publishing house Flammarion (1953–1961) and finally for the Société française de documentation (1962–68). In 1955 he was employed by the Rapho agency, and from 1968 on he worked as an independent photographer in Paris. He has numerous publications of books of photographs with Balland Publications including: *Métamorphoses de Paris* (1967 and 1976), *Métamorphoses de la banlieu* (1969), and *Métamorphoses de la Côte d'Azur* (1970).

COBURN Alvin Langdon (1882–1966)
Born in Boston (U.S.A.) he became one of the most important photographers of the pictorial movement. He began making photographs when he was 16 years old, and frequented the circle connected with *Camera Work*, Stieglitz's journal, which published Coburn's first photograph in 1904. He interested himself with effects of fog, smoke, light and shade; his compositions are relatively modern. He photographed landscapes in the USA and in England, as well as making a number of portraits of intellectuals of the time (Shaw, Pound, Twain). Inspired by the cubists, Coburn produced abstract photographs in 1917: the *Vortographes*. In 1909 he published *London*, in 1910 *New York*, and in 1913 *Men of Mark*. After having produced some photographic reports, his vertiginous scenes illustrate a desire to demonstrate "a freedom of expression, without which art can do nothing."

COUPPIER Jules
Couppier was a chemist by profession, and a member of the Société française de photographie. He appears to have specialized in stereoscopic photography around 1854, of which he exhibited a few views in Brussels in 1856. He established his studio first in the rue Saint-Victor (1857–58) and then in the rue Contrescarpe-Saint-Marcel (1859–1861).

DAGUERRE Louis-Jacques Mandé (1787–1851)
Daguerre was born in Cormeilles-en-Parisis. A painter and stage designer, in 1822 he opened the Diorama in Paris, a trompe-l'oeil spectacle full of subtle light games, set up on the current site of the barracks of the Republican guards in the Place de la République. As one of those attempting to make permanent the images of the camera obscura, he became associated with Nicéphore Niepce—the inventor of photography—in 1829. After Niepce's death in 1833, Daguerre pursued his researches alone, and in 1838 made the first successful daguerréotypes. His discovery was announced to the Académie des Sciences on January 7, 1839, by deputy Arago, and on August 19, Arago, speaking on behalf of the government, authorized the process for general use. Daguerre received a substantial award which allowed him to retire and live in Bry-sur-Marne. His *Historique et description des procédés de daguerréotypie et du diorama* (1839) went through 30 editions in all languages, in 18 months!

DAVIDSON Bruce (1933)
Davidson was born in Chicago (U.S.A.), of Polish extraction. He began photographing at the age of ten. Upon finishing high school he enrolled at the Rochester Institute of Technology, where he discovered the work of Frank, Smith and Cartier-Bresson. His first photo essay was published by *Life* in 1954. In 1956 he joined the general quarters of the Allied Forces near Paris which he visited every weekend and where he became acquainted with the "Widow Montmartre." He joined the Magnum agency in 1958 and began a series of photo essays. He worked for *Vogue*, *Esquire*, *Life* and *Queen*. In 1962 he was awarded a Guggenheim grant and covered the "Freedom March" for the *New York Times*. He began teach-

ing photography from his own studio in 1964. Following this he made other documentaries, in the South and, above all, in Harlem in 1966; documentaries which were given concrete form in *East 100th Street* (1970). Davidson has also produced several shorts for movies and television. He lives in New York.

DEMACHY Robert (1859–1936)
Born in Saint-Germain-en-Laye (Yvelines) Demachy was a rich, well-read banker and amateur artist, who from 1892 on devoted himself primarily to photography. He became a member of the Société française de photographie (1882), was a founding member of Photo-club de Paris, a party leader of the pictorial school, and a convinced partisan of artistic techniques in which elimination plays the main role (for example the use of bichromated gum which he improved, or the oil transfer technique which he invented). For Demachy "the work of art is not in the motif but in its presentation." Stieglitz published his works in *Camera Work* and exhibited them in New York in 1904. Demachy wrote a number of technical books. He abandoned photography in 1914.

DOISNEAU Robert (1912)
Doisneau was born in Gentilly. After his studies at the Ecole Estienne, he became assistant to André Vigneau in 1931. He sold his first photograph to the journal *Excelsior* in 1932, and began work for the photographic service of the Renault factories. Once licensed, he began working on his own. He joined the Rapho agency in 1945. After a brief contract with *Vogue*, began a period of acquaintance with interesting figures such as Cendrars and Baguet and of grand Parisian rambles with Giraud and Prévert. Doisneau published countless essays in the greater number of illustrated magazines. He won the Kodak Prize in 1947, and the Niepce Prize in 1956. He has exhibited in major international museums, and his principal publications include: *Banlieue de Paris* (Seghers, 1949), *Instantanés de Paris* (Artaud, 1955), *Les Parisiens tels qu'ils sont* (Delpire, 1954), *Le Paris de Doisneau et Max Pol Fouchet* (1974), and *Trois secondes d'éternité* (Contrejour, 1979). The most Parisian of photographers, his images, full of poetry, humor and humanity have already become classics of humanist documentation.

DONTENVILLE
Little is known of this photographer, whose studio was located on the rue de Charonne. He photographed Paris, especially the Louvre, the Tuileries and the pavilions of the 1867 Universal Exhibition.

ERWITT Elliott (1928)
Born in Paris, he and his family fled from fascism, emigrating to America in 1939. He studied at Hollywood High School and began photographing in New York in 1948. He worked with Roy Stryker at Standard Oil in 1949, and by 1951 was with the military in France. Steichen selected certain of his photos for inclusion in the *Family of Man*. He worked in fashion and advertising, joining Magnum in 1958. His photographs have been published in most important periodicals and exhibited in numerous galleries and museums. He is the author of: *Photographie et anti-photographie* (1972), *Chiens de ma chienne* (Chêne, 1974), and *Récents Développements* (1978). Since 1970 he has produced numerous short films. A master of visual puns, his photographs constitute a human comedy similar to Chaplin's.

FERRIER
The Ferriers Claude-Marie Ferrier (father) and Jacques-Alexandre (son) associated themselves with Soulier in order to establish a studio on the Boulevard de Sébastopol specializing in the sale and publishing of stereoscopic plates. Their catalogue, published in 1864, offered to the public photographs of countries the world over and, of course, of Paris. They were among the principal producers of these plates, which were the rage in Paris and France during the 1850s.

FOURNEAUX Lionel (1954)
Fourneaux was born in Suresnes (Haut de Seine). He pursued his secondary and higher studies until 1977 when, after a new university orientation (audio visual techniques) and certain personal encounters, he began to teach himself photography. He was a stringer for the Moba Presse agency in 1981 and 1982 and has participated in various group shows, including the Mois de la Photo in Paris (1980). He was a fellow of the Fondation nationale de la photographie in 1979 and received the young photographer award at the Rencontres internationales d'Ariles in 1979.

FRANCK Martine (1938)
Franck was born in Antwerp (The Netherlands). She attended elementary school in the U.S.A., secondary school in England, and university in Madrid and Paris (Ecole de Louvre from 1958 to 1962). She began to photograph in the Far East in 1963, and worked in the photo lab at *Time Life* in 1964. She worked independently for *Life*, *Fortune*, the *New York Times*, and *Vogue*, and then for the theater cooperative Théâtre du Soleil as a photographer. She was a member of the Vu agency in 1970–71, and became a co-founder of Viva in 1972. She joined Magnum in 1980, and has had a number of solo and group shows in France and abroad. Publications: *Martine Franck* (Contrejour, 1976), *Quartier Beauborg* (Centre Pompidou, 1977), *Les Lubérons* (Chêne, 1978), *Le Temps de vieillir* (Filipacchi—Denoêl, 1980), and *Le Théâtre de Soleil* (Double Page, 1982). R. Doisneau states that Martine Franck's photography puts into practice "a friendly eye, a single attitude establishing the mutual exchange of confidence and respect which one can read in her images." Her images are direct, refined, tinged with humor and full of poetry.

GAUMY Jean (1948)
Born in Royan, Gaumy was an editor and photographer for *Paris Normandie* from 1969 to 1972. In 1972 he gave his photos to the Viva agency for distribution, and in 1973 he began work for the famous Gamma agency where he remained for four years. He joined Magnum in 1977. Gaumy favours long investigative essays covering prisons, hospitals, deep-sea fishermen etc. He is the author of: *L'Hôpital* (Contrejour, 1976) and *Les Incarcérés* (Ed. de l'Etoile, 1984).

GAUTRAND Jean-Claude (1932)
Born in Sains-en-Gohelle (Pas-de-Calais), Gautrand was self-taught. He began to photograph in 1959. A co-founder of the group "libres expressions" in 1964, he was also a member and vice-president of "30 × 40." Critic and editor of many specialized French periodicals, he has written extensively on photography. His photographs have been published and exhibited all over France and elsewhere. He won the Grand Prix des Arts de la Ville de Marseille from the Musée Cantini in 1968. He is a member of the advisory board of the Fondation Nationale de la Photographie and

secretary-general of the Nadar Prize association. Publications: *Les Murs de mai* (1968), *L'Assassinat de Baltard* (1972), and *Les Forteresses du dérisoire* (1977). His photographs have a lyrical quality and are always thematic, focusing on subjects with rich graphic qualities, which nonetheless allow an obvious social engagement to shine through.

GAUTRAND Philippe (1969)
Born in Paris, Gautrand created his first images at the age of six with an Instamatic. Since 1980, encouraged by Brassaï, he has been photographing the streets of Paris and the countryside of Paris seen from above.

GOUVIOT A.
This still relatively unknown photographer is the author of a magnificent album preserved in the Bibliothèque historique de la Ville de Paris comprising 12 views of the city gates built by the architect Ledoux. This collection is entitled *l'Enceinte de Paris jusqu'en 1859*.

GUEUVIN A.
Gueuvin moved to the Boulevards des Italiens in Paris in 1851 and, from 1863 to 1867 had a large portrait studio on the rue Cassette. Little is known of this photographer apart from a series of photographs of the principal monuments in Paris, made in 1864–65. With Bonoldi, he also produced a series of panoramas using Koch's camera between 1867 and 1871.

HARBUTT Charles (1935)
Born in Camden (U.S.A.), Harbutt pursued his studies at the University of Marquette. From 1956 on he was co-editor of *Jubilee Magazine*, doing the writing and photographing for socially oriented essays on migrant workers and southerners. In 1959 he went free-lance, making essays on Cuba, New York, the blind, Wall Street. In 1963 he joined the Magnum agency and worked for *Look*, *Life*, *Newsweek*, *Paris Match*, *Stern*, *Epoca*, and others. In 1970 he began teaching at several large universities and has had many shows in major international museums. Publications: *América in Cris* (1969); *Travelog* (1974) received the book award at the Arles Festival. Harbutt's photos balance between abstraction and document, the real and surreal. His work belongs to the school of "the banal reality" which flourished in the USA during the seventies.

HERVE Lucien (1910)
He was born in Hungary and settled in Paris in 1929. A prisoner in 1941, he escaped and went to work for the resistance. In 1947 he was hired as a reporter for *France illustration*. He was sent to Marseille by *Plaisir de France* to photograph Le Corbusier's apartment building. The magazine's editorial board refused to publish his photos, but the famous architect liked them and asked him to become his photographer, a position which he filled until Le Corbusier's death. He participated in many exhibitions, among them "Le Langage de l'architecture" at the Musée des Arts Décoratifs in Paris (1964), and in various French and European cities, especially at the abbey of Royaumont (1969) and then in 1974, the exhibition "Une Ville Nouvelle au XVIe siècle" which traveled in Europe and the U.S.A. His main preoccupations were with the discovery of the emotional aspects of insignificant objects, and with the importance of integrating architectural forms into the environment. Publications: *La Plus Grande Aventure du*

monde (Arthaud, 1956), *Photo et Architecture; Le Beau court la rue* (1970), and *Le Corbusier* (Ed. Griffon, 1970).

HOSSARD
Hossard was a professor at the Ecole Polytechnique and a friend of Daguerre. Of his works, only the series of daguerreotypes made on the banks of the Seine are known. The Kodak Foundation presented them to the Musée d'Orsay.

IZIS (1911–1980)
(Real name: Israëlis Biedermanas). He was born in Lithuania, learned photography around 1924, and arrived in Paris in 1930. The following year he opened a shop on the rue Nationale, in the 13th arrondissement. In 1944, the war forced him to take refuge in the Limousin. In 1944 he participated in the liberation of Limoges, joined the FFI and photographed the resistance group "Ceux de Grammont." In 1946 he returned to the capital and exhibited photos of Paris, which were to form the core of his book *Paris des rêves* (Ed. Claire-Fontaine, 1949). Beginning in 1949 he worked for *Match* as a stringer, and photographed Chagall painting the ceiling of the Opéra. He had many exhibitions, including those at the Museum of Modern Art in New York (1952), Chicago (1955), Tel Aviv (1972), and Arles (1978). His major publications are: *Bal du printemps* with text by Prévert (Ed. Claire-Fontaine, 1951), *Le Cirque d'Izis* (1965), *Le Monde de Chagall* (Gallimard, 1969), and *Paris des poètes* (Nathan, 1977). He was one of the most authentic poets of photography fascinated by Paris. His tender, simple images leave ample room for dreams.

JACQUES René (1908)
(Real name: René Giton). Born in Phnom Pehn (Cambodia), he made his first photos in 1925 and became a photo illustrator in 1930. His work was published in numerous pre-war journals, particularly in the famous annual albums of *Arts et Métiers graphiques*, and he has exhibited in Paris and New York (Museum of Modern Art, 1937). He became known as a subtle photographer of Paris with *Envoûtement de Paris* published in 1938 with text by F. Carco (Ed. Grasset), and enjoyed a reputation as a photographer of the stage in 1938–39. He became a member of the group Rectangle founded by Sougez in 1941 and in 1946 of the Groupe des XV. In 1945 he created an advertising and illustration division for the Syndicat des Graphistes Publicitaires. He illustrated an enormous quantity of tourist and documentary books, as well as advertising pamphlets, until 1975, at which time he ceased working. He participated in the retrospective *Paris 1950 photographié par le Groupe des XV* held at the Bibliothèque historique de la Ville de Paris in 1983 and showed a grand retrospective of his work at the Fondation nationale de la photographie in Lyon (1984). An exceptional technician, René-Jacques' simplicity and his ability to capture the fugitive, created timeless images based on the harmony of forms and the quality of light which go right to the heart of daily life.

JARRE Louis
We have no documentation concerning this photographer.

KERTÉSZ André (1894–1985)
Kertész was born in Budapest (Hungary) and studied at the Academy of Business. He then accepted a position with the Stock Exchange in 1912. With his first savings, he bought a camera.

In 1915 he joined the Austro-Hungarian army and made a lengthy photo essay of which a few photographs were published in the press, while others were destroyed at the time of the 1918 revolution. After the war, he decided to become a photographer, and in 1925 arrived in Paris and settled in Montparnasse. He produced many photos of streets, as well as artists portraits. In 1927 he had his first solo exhibition (Galerie Sacre du Printemps). In 1928 he bought his first Leica and worked for *Vu* and other periodicals. Exhibitions of his works followed one another; in Stuttgart *Film und Foto*; in Essen *Photographie Contemporaine* (1929); in New York (1932). In 1933 he produced his famous *Distorsions*. In 1936 he arrived in New York. The war forced him to remain in the U.S.A. where he worked for *Harper's Bazaar, Look, Vogue* and *Collier's*. His photographs of interiors and fashion were well received, but his essays remained misunderstood. He signed an exclusive contract with Condé Nast in New York from 1949 to 1952. In 1962 he broke all of his contracts and began making photographs to satisfy himself only. In 1963 he won the golden medal at the Biennial in Venice, and he had solo shows at the Bibliothèque Nationale (Paris, 1963), the Museum of Modern Art (New York, 1964), and the Centre Georges Pompidou (Paris, 1977). He received the Legion d'Honneur and the Grand Prix National de la Photo in 1983. Publications: *Paris vu par André Kertész* (Plon, 1934), *Nos amis les bêtes* (Plon, 1936), *Day of Paris* (NY, 1945), *Lectures* (Chêne, 1971), *André Kertész, Soixante ans de photographies* (Chêne, 1972), *Distorsions* (Chêne, 1976) and *A ma fenêtre* (Herscher, 1982). A permanent curiosity, a sense of forms and of the unusual, an original vision, a sensitive approach to man and things, make Kertész a master "to whom we all owe something" (H. Cartier-Bresson). He remains one of the greatest figures, if not the greatest, in the history of photography.

KOLLAR François (1904–1979)
Born in Hungary, Kollar arrived when he was 16 years old in Paris, a city he was never to leave. He worked at making art reproductions for the Bernes firm, and there he met many artists. He then became the studio head with Draeger. The Horizons de France charged him with the illustration of *La France travaille*, a work with a preface by Paul Valéry (a project involving three years' work, and 10,000 photos). He also worked with other French and foreign magazines, including: *Plaisir de France, Art Vivant, Vu, Figaro illustré, Silberspiegel*. In 1931 he began work as a photographer for *Harper's Bazaar*—a relationship which lasted for sixteen years. He exhibited frequently alongside Man Ray, Kertész, Vigneau, Landau, and Moral. After the war he worked in advertising. He discovered, and became passionate about, color photography. He made two more extensive photo essays, one in Africa and the other in the U.S.A. Since his disappearance in 1979, exhibitions in Paris, Arles and in Czechoslovakia have paid homage to his work.

LACHEROY Henry (1884–1960)
Lacheroy was born in Annecy. After his apprenticeship he made shots for postcards in 1896. Around 1905 he was a retoucher and portraitist. He worked as a photographer in the Michelin factories from 1919 to 1924. In 1938 he entered the service of a Hamburg banker and began to build up a private clientele. In 1920 he was awarded first prize in the competition for the best worker in France in photography. He became a professor at the Ecole de Vaugirard and was a member of the Groupe des XV from 1946 to 1948. He published in *Arts et Métiers graphiques*, *L'Illustration*, and

Acier. One of the greatest French industrial photographers, he knew how to create graphic images bordering on abstraction, where originality of layout and subtle use of light bear witness to a fascination for technological objects.

LE DIASCORN François (1947)
Le Diascorn studied political science and received a law degree. He began to photograph in 1971, and made his first trip to India. In 1972 and 1973 he worked as a photographer and cameraman for an American television network. He traveled to Mexico. From 1973 to 1976, he worked in advertising, when he left to cover the United States bicentennial. In 1978 he joined the Viva agency in Paris. The following year he received a grant from the Fondation nationale de la photographie and was part of the section "Jeune Photographie Française" in Arles. He produced a long essay on the group Urban Sax for the exhibition *Photoscopie 81*. Since then he has traveled extensively, mostly in the U.S.A.

LE GRAY Gustave (1820–1882)
Le Gray was born in Villiers-le-Bel. As a painter he exhibited his works in the Salons of 1848 and 1853, but it was in the area of photography that he excelled. An excellent chemist, he was interested in the sensitivity of emulsions, and in 1851 he invented the waxed paper process. He used this process while carrying out a commission from the Mission Héliographique which he undertook with Mestral in Touraine and Aquitaine. He developed the collodion process, which he described in numerous treatises. As a teacher he inspired various figures, including Le Secq, Nègre, and Tournachon. He tried his hand at the reportage and the landscape, with great skill. Scorning the mercantile aspects of industrial photography, he refused to adapt himself to the new style of portraiture, namely the "calling card" introduced by Disderi. He preferred to relinquish his studio on the Boulevard des Capucines and left for Cairo where he taught drawing. He was a founding member of the Société française de photographie.

LEON Auguste
Very little is known of this photographer who was one of the team of reporters and film makers charged by the financier Albert Kahn to make the "archives de la planète" intended to preserve "once and for all the aspects, practices and styles of human activity whose total disappearance is only a question of time." The material for this gigantic enterprise is today carefully preserved in the Albert Kahn photo and film library. He was to make 72,000 *autochromes*, of which more than 5,000 are of Paris, between 1910 and 1931. A complete record, thanks to the magic of the Lumière brothers' process, it offers a captivating view of the Parisian landscape and activities around the years of the First World War. Recruited in 1910, Auguste Lèon was one of the first two operators of a team, certain of whose members have remained anonymous.

LE SECQ Henri (1818–1882)
Born in Paris, Le Secq was a painter of small talent. He discovered photography in 1848 after having studied with Le Gray. His calotypes of architecture executed for the Mission Héliographique, and then for himself, are magnificent. A certain number of his views of the monuments of Paris were published in several albums by Blanquart-Evrard. He was the author of a collection entitled *Photographies relatives aux travaux de la Ville de Paris* (1849–1853), as well as of an

exceptional series of still lives (1855–1856) and a number of no less astonishing series of landscapes of the Normandy coast around Dieppe. He abandoned photography around 1856 and devoted himself to his collection of iron-work, today observed in Rouen. He was the gifted prototype of the school of 1850's French calotypists who were completely indifferent to the growing intrusion of business into the photographic milieu.

MAN RAY (1890–1976)
Born in Philadelphia, U.S.A., Man Ray studied architecture and engineering. He started painting in 1910, and, in 1911, became interested in photography at the famous gallery opened by Stieglitz in New York. From 1915 onward he was one of the most dynamic representatives of New York Dadaism. In 1920 he and Duchamp founded the "Anonymous Society" to promote modern art. Man Ray arrived in Paris in 1921, where he met Picabia, Tzara, and Breton. By placing objects on sensitized paper, he discovered "rayography", with which he made numerous photographs of surrealist writers, painters, and nudes. In 1930 he rediscovered solarization, and applied it to his work on portraits. After living in Hollywood from 1940 to 1950, he returned to Paris. His passionate *Autoportraits* was published in 1963 (Laffont). Exhibitions of his paintings, sculpture, and photographs have appeared in many of the large international museums.
Man Ray makes use of almost all of the techniques and creative materials accessible to the spirit and the hand of man. Taking a permanent joy in creating, he demonstrates the richness of his inspiration, the diversity of his invention, and an astonishing spiritual resourcefulness. "I paint the things I'm not allowed to photograph, and I photograph the things I'm not allowed to paint," he said.

MARTENS Friedrich von (circa 1809–1875)
An engraver and photographer of German origin, Martens was born in Venice and settled in Paris in the 1840s. He employed daguerréotypes, some of which, engraved by Lerebours, were included in the *Excursions daguerriennes*. Later he used the collodion in his work. In 1845, Martens constructed the first panoramic camera which permitted a visual angle of more than 150 degrees. The lens pivoted on a vertical axis in front of a curved, mobile, 12 by 40 centimeter, plate. In the company of Colonel Langlois, he made a photo report on the Crimean War (1854–1856). In 1855, he made some extraordinary mountain photographs, in particular of Mont Blanc.

MARTIN André (1928)
Born in Normandy, Martin studied in Rouen and received a diploma in cinematography at the Vaugirard School in 1950. Soon after, he abandoned the cinema in favor of photography. He worked in many areas: reporting, landscapes, animals and architecture, alternating happily between assignments on large publicity campaigns and personal research. His work appeared in many publications and periodicals. At least fifteen of his collections were published by Delpire, including *Chambord* and *Kairouan* (1963); *Tout Paris* (1964); *Toute la Normandie* and *La Tour Eiffel* (1965); *L'Insecte* (1968); *Image d'une France* (1977); as well as *Les Noires Vallees de repentir* (Entente, 1977), which won the prix Nadar; and *l'Opera de Paris* (Photopoche, 1985).

MARVILLE Charles (1816–1879)
Painter, engraver, and designer of the 1840s, Marville's first photographs were published in

1851 in the Blanquard-Evrard *Album photographique de l'artiste et de l'amateur, Mélanges photographiques*, and *Paris photographique*. In 1852 he undertook a photographic excursion in the north of France and a long trip through Germany, photographing several large cathedrals before returning to make calotypes in the area between Strasbourg and Riems. Marville's latest photographs were published by Blanquard-Evrard in numerous collections of which the last, in 1854, is devoted to the banks of the Rhine. Back with his painting friends in the Barbizon, he photographed landscapes and plants. He took part in all of the Paris Exhibitions, and the London Exhibition of 1862, where he was awarded the silver medal. In 1858 he produced an album on the Bois de Boulogne. Named the "Photographer of Paris", he began his enormous collection of photographs of the old streets and districts of Paris during the time of the demolitions under Haussmann. Step by step, he documented the extensive new construction of motorways. In 1872, he was given another mission: to photograph the restoration of cathedrals and monuments.
Having always refused to be drawn into photographic commercialism, Marville has left us a body of work precious among other things for its record of the Parisian heritage, providing an unforgettable vision of Paris under the second empire.

MASCLET Daniel (1892–1969)
Born in Blois, as a youngster he studied the cello, and won a Conservatoire prize at the age of 17. Interrupted by the 1914 war, his career as a professional musician was resumed in 1918. In 1920, he met R. Demachy, who introduced him to Baron de Meyer, the great fashion photographer, whose assistant he became until 1925. From 1925 to 1928 he worked with *Vogue*, at that time under the direction of Lucien Vogel. In 1928 he moved to the Île Saint-Louis, where he devoted himself completely to his art. He took a stand against the current preoccupation, pictorialism, and favored "photographie pure", as he concentrated more and more on portraits and landscapes. His numerous writings, his talks, his published collections, are all imbued with the aura of an authentic photographer, and endowed with an unforgettable perfection of technique. Perfectionist, polemicist, and philosopher, he was a leading light at the meetings of the "30 by 40", the Parisian photography club. He took part in innumerable exhibitions either as contributor or member of the jury. In 1933 he created the Salon du Nu. Publications: *Nus* (Brown, 1934); *le Paysage en Photographie, le Portrait* (1969).

MAUBAN
We have no documentation on this artist.

MONIER Albert (1910)
Born in the Cantal, Monier studied in Rouen. At the age of 17, he entered his father's furniture business and began collecting picture postcards. He bought his first camera in 1928 and began photographing everyday things and the people around him. Then, tired of business, he left for Morocco to become a professional photographer. Commercial failure caused his return to Paris in 1950. He decided to make postcards of the quais, the sidewalks, and Parisian folklore. It took him fifteen days to make the first series of pictures which he developed in an old cottage in Cantal without water, and sold from door to door to Parisian newsagents. In spite of these particularly difficult beginnings, the venture was soon a success, and millions of postcards were sold. In 1960 he

published a series of universal themes, and in 1962, a series of photographic posters. He retired in 1970. Shunning all the fashions and schools, Albert Monier has fought the fight of a craftsman to distribute simple pictures destined for the public at large. He is in fact the inventor of the modern postcard, and helped to foster the craze for these small pictures which have been collected and cherished ever since. Publications: *Paris* (1950), *Au pays des Grandes Causses* (1959), and *Albert Monier photographe* (Aurillac, 1983).

MUNOZ DE PABLOS Angel (1931)
Born in Algete-Madrid (Spain), Munoz de Pablos became interested in photography in 1958. From 1958 to 1961 he studied at the State College of Photography in Cologne. In 1961 he covered industrial subjects in Belgium. Two years later he moved to Paris and worked in the laboratory of the National Archives. In 1967 he became an independent photo-journalist. In 1983 he did freelance work for the Explorer Agency. His work has appeared in various publications including *Plaisir de France*, and *l'Express*, and has been exhibited in Cologne, Spain (1962), at the Museum of Modern Art in Paris, the Club "30 by 40" (1965), Théâtre Récamier (1978), and the World Press Photo (1969).

NEGRE Charles (1820–1880)
Born in Grasse (France), Nègre studied painting in the de la Roche Atelier and at the Ecole des Beaux Artes in Paris. In 1844, he made his first daguerréotypes, but continued to paint and exhibit at the Salon. In 1848 he began making photographs on paper. From 1851 to 1854 he photographed the Île Saint Louis, concentrating on the ordinary people, street scenes, and markets. In 1854 he produced the first plates of his *Midi de la France*, and in 1859, a complete photo essay on l'Asile impérial de Vincennes. He was very interested in techniques for transforming photographs into engraved plates. In 1860 he went to live in Nice. Charles Nègre, one of the most brilliant calotypists, may well have been one of the first to understand the unique contribution to be made by photography in capturing everyday life. His remarkable compositions bear witness to his interest in humanity. He was a founding member of the SFP (Société française de photographie).

PERCEVAL Alain (1933)
Born in Lyon, Perceval learned photography from his grandparents. He first photographed mountain views at the age of 16. He began a military career in 1953, first in the Alpine Hunters, and later (1954–1959) as a navigational photographer. He eventually became a photography instructor at the School of Military Aviation at Nancy. While in charge of research at the army experimental center, he made detailed studies of shooting techniques. When he returned to civilian life, he began working in the Spirale society. He was a notable specialist in aerial photography, making many series of quality picture-postcards for tourists, as well as prospectuses and posters for the Commission of Tourism, for which he was awarded two Oscars in the United States. He produced important illustrations for school textbooks and various collections, of which the most important remains *La France* (Arthaud).

PUYO Emile Joachim Constant (1857–1933)
Puyo studied at the Polytechnic and then at a military high school. Later, in the military, he participated in campaigns in South Oranais. He was a

squadron commander at the school of artillery, and became interested in photography at the Universal Exhibition of 1899. From 1902 on, he devoted himself entirely to photography in his studio in Paris, Vincennes, then upon retiring in 1926, in Morlaix. A great lover of the art, he became one of the leaders and theorists of pictorialism. With Demachy and Bocquet, he was a leading light in the famous Paris Photoclub, and a typical representative of the monied bourgeois class, with no need to market his work. He prioritized the intervention of the artist in the creative process. He was an enthusiast of the pigmentary processes: rubber, oil, and transfers of all kinds. In 1906 he published *Camera Work*. Numerous theoretical articles followed in the sumptuous *Revue de photographie* (1903–1908), which he founded, and also in technical books: *Les Procédés d'arts* (1906), *Les Procédés aux encres grasses* (1923), and works on portrait and landscape photography (1925).

RAIMOND-DITYVON Claude (1941)

Born in la Rochelle, Dityvon came to Paris in 1962 where he became passionately interested in the great classic cinematographers, including Vigo, Keaton, Eisenstein and von Stroheim, and in Japanese and American films. He expressed an admiration for Robert Frank and Henri Cartier-Bresson. He obtained the prix Niepce in 1970, co-founded the Viva agency in 1972, and in 1973, with this group, participated in the exhibition called *The Family in France*. In 1972 he produced a solo exhibition for the Museum of Modern Art in Paris, and participated in numerous group exhibitions. His publications include *Dityvon* (Creatais-Viva, 1978), *Gens de la Rochelle* (Contrejour, 1979), *Dityvon, 59 auteurs de bandes dessinées* (Futuropolis, 1981). Dityvon's pictures contain nothing anecdotal or picturesque for its own sake. Reduced as they are to the bare bones of an idea, they are perfectly constructed around a certain number of people who share the picture without knowing one another.

RIBOUD Marc (1923)

Born in Lyon, Riboud studied at the Central School of Lyon. He produced his first photographs at the Universal Exhibition in Paris in 1937. During the war he joined the resistance at the Maquis in Vercors, and once the war was over, completed his engineering studies. The photographs he took at the festivals of Lyon and Avignon in 1951 were published in *Art et Théâtre de France*. That same year, he met Cartier-Bresson and decided to devote himself completely to photography. The dam and the disappearance of the village of Taignes was the subject of his first photographic essay. In 1952 he joined the Magnum agency, and took his famous photograph of the painter on the Eiffel Tower which was published in *Life*. In 1955 he traveled extensively in the Indies, China, Africa, Vietnam, the United States, Poland and Cuba. In 1976 he was chosen president of Magnum Photo, which he left in 1979. On two occasions he was awarded prizes by the Overseas Press Club. His work appeared in innumerable publications in all of the international periodicals, as well as exhibitions in various parts of the world, including the Art Institute of Chicago, ICP, and the Museum of Modern Art in Paris. His collections include *Ghana* (1964), *Les Trois Barriers de Chine* (Laffonte, 1966), and *Chine, Instantanes de Voyage* (Arthaud, 1980). It is above all in his remarkable formal compositions that Riboud bears passionate and tender witness to mankind.

RONIS Willy (1910)

Ronis was born in Paris, where he studied music. He took his first photographs on holiday in 1926, and soon after began to photograph Paris. In 1936 he became a photo-reporter and a freelance illustrator. He worked for Recontre Chim and his first photo essay appeared in *Plaisir de France*. In 1938–39 he photographed the strikes at Citroën. In 1943–44 he returned to the free zone, and after liberation worked for *Life* and other periodicals. He was a member of Groupe des XV, and joined the Rapho agency. He won the Kodak prize in 1947, and was a gold medalist of the Venice Biennial of 1957. During the Sixties he produced illustrations for numerous publications as well as collected works, including a photo essay on Algiers. In 1972 he moved from Paris to the south of France and taught at the universities of Aix-en-Provence and Marseilles. He won the Grand Prix de artes et des lettres in 1979, and was the guest of honor at the Arles festival in 1980. He was awarded the Nadar prize in 1981 for his album *Sur le fil du hazard* (Contrejour). In 1983 he gave his work to the state and returned to Paris. In 1984 *Belleville-Menilmontant* was reissued by Arthaud. Ronis was a true representative of the French school of humanist photo-essayists; his images of Paris and of other places constitutes a caring personal chronicle of the life of man.

SALAÜN Philippe (1943)

Born in Brittany, Salaün began work as a photographic assistant in an advertising studio. In 1969 he became an apprentice in a professional laboratory, but returned to advertising after a year. In 1971 he joined a professional laboratory as a fine artist. In 1979, after his debut, he created the atelier Philippe Salaün, which received a grant from the National Photographic Foundation in 1980. He has participated regularly in the organization of technical workshops, and exhibits around the world.

SEEBERGER

Jules (1872–1932), Louis (1874–1946), and Henri (1876–1956). The brothers founded a veritable dynasty of photographers. They began their schooling in Lyon and then in Paris, studying design at the School of Bernard Palissy. In 1898 Jules took his first photographs of Montmartre while Henri founded a design studio. They both took part in the annual competitions of the City of Paris from 1904 to 1907 and their work was first published in *l'Illustration* in 1905. Their postcards of Montmartre were published in 1906 at the request of L. Berger, the illustrated postcard firm. Jules and Henri, soon to be joined by Louis, began their series of shots of French towns. One year later, a tour of France complete, the Seebergers received the gold medal at the Exhibition of the City of Paris. They also exhibited at the Palais des Glace with the pictorialists, and pursued their work in this field until 1914. From 1908 on they provided *Mode* with photo essays on fashion and the fashionable world, and also worked for the most celebrated couturiers. The Seebergers's work appeared in numerous international publications. In 1910 their first autochromes appeared in a photo-essay on the floods in Paris. The birth of Jean, then of Albert four years later marked the beginning of a new generation of Seebergers. After the 1914–1918 war, Jules abandoned photography, while his two brothers continued to photograph the fashionable world for *Jardin des Modes*, *Vu*, *Adam*, *Harper's Bazaar*, and *Noir et Blanc*. In 1923 a Hollywood agency assigned the photographing of Paris to the Seebergers to allow the Hollywood studios to reconstruct the scenery of la vie Parisienne, a task which lated until 1931. Jean and Albert followed in their fathers's footsteps. Mobilized in 1935, when they returned after the fall of France, they went straight to Paris and took up the work of the studio. They produced photographs of the occupation of Paris, then of the Paris of the liberation, as well as fashion personalities. Members of the Groupe des XV, their studio on the Boulevard Bon Marche was finally closed on the first of April, 1977. A family which, in devoting itself to photography, has enriched the national heritage, leaving a magnificent mirror of the France of the beginning of the century, and of life in the Belle Epoque.

SIEFF Jean-loup (1933)

Born in Paris, Sieff completed secondary school and went on to get his baccalaureate in philosophy. He took his first photographs at the age of 15, and began work in 1954 as a freelance photo-journalist, producing many photo-essays without publication. Engaged in 1955 by *Elle* as a photo-reporter, and then as a fashion photographer, he resigned in 1958 to join the Magnum Agency, which he left in 1959. He took assignments from *Réalités* and *Jardin de Modes*, and won the Prix Niepce in 1959. He moved to New York in 1961. Sieff worked in Europe for *Glamour*, *Harper's Bazaar*, *Look*, *Esquire*, then for *Vogue*, *Twen*, *Elle*, and *Queen*. He returned to Paris in 1966. His work has appeared in numerous exhibitions in the large international museums, and in 1978 he became director of the collection "Journal d'une voyage" (de Noel). His publications include *La Vallée de la mort* (de Noel, 1978), *Best of Nudes* (Tokyo, 1980), *Portraits de Dames assises, de paysages tristes et des nus mollement las . . .* (Contrejour, 1982). Thanks to the formal quality of his photographs, the diversity of his backgrounds, and the effective use of the wide angle lenses and contrast, Sieff's photographs have had an enormous impact on the content of the contemporary photographic vision.

SOUGEZ Emmanuel (1889–1972)

Born in Bordeaux, Sougez began working in photography at the age of 13 at l'Ecole des beaux-arts in Bordeaux in 1904. He arrived in Paris in 1911, quit the official course and traveled through Europe. In 1919 he became well-known as a photo-illustrator, taking charge of the photographic service of *l'Illustration* in 1926, a job he kept until the title was discontinued. He became one of the key personages in photography between the wars, and a leader of the movement for "photographie pure" in France. He was a founder of the group Rectangle. From 1930 to 1936 he published the best contemporary photos in the annual photographic supplements of *Arts et Métiers graphiques*. He was well known for his portraits, landscapes and his art photography, but was also the author of personal studies on the object, material, and light. As an historian and theorist, his activity was multifarious. He founded the Groupe des XV in 1946. His publications include many illustrated collections on the art of the large international museums: *la Photographie et son histoire* (Illustration, 1968), and *la Photographie et son univers* (Illustration, 1969). The absolute rigor of Sougez's pictures is the fruit of a process of composition verging on perfection and of an exceptional technique which permits him a total command of his material. Endowed with a particularly refined sensibility, his theories are akin to those of Weston and Ranger Pastch.

SOULIER Charles (before 1840–after 1875)

Soulier started work with Clouzard in 1854 and joined Ferrier in 1859 to open an establishment on the Boulevard Sebastopol, specializing in the publication and sale of stereoscopic pictures. His extensive catalog offers documents of the greatest diversity, both internationally and at home. In 1869 he made a series of plates of a climb of

Mont-Blanc, following it up with three beautiful series of mountain photos. His numerous exhibitions appeared in Paris (1861, 63, 64, 65, 69), Amsterdam, 1862), Berlin (1869), Brussels (1857), and London (1858).

STIEGLITZ Alfred (1864–1946)

Born in Hoboken, New Jersey (U.S.A.), Stieglitz attended secondary school in New York, and continued his studies in Berlin in engineering from 1882–90. During this time he took his first photographs, began writing for photographic periodicals, exhibiting his work, and entering it in competitions. In 1890, back in the U.S.A., he worked in photogravure, making use of his spare time photographing in the street, with the use of his "detective". In 1891 he became a member of the Society for Amateur Photographers, becoming the editor in chief of its bulletin. Adopting the motto "explore the familiar", he preached a different kind of photography, making pictures indoors, in snow and rain storms. He organized numerous exhibitions and in 1896 became vice president of the Camera Club and editor in chief of its bulletin, *Camera Notes*. He founded in 1902 the movement Photo-Secession with the object of improving the position of photography as a "pictorial expression". Stieglitz mounted an exhibition devoted to American pictorial photography, in which he presented to the public the photos of nonconformists like Steichen, Bullock, White, Coburn, all of whom were closely akin to pictorialism. He also founded the most resplendent of the reviews on the history of photography, *Camera Work*, which was soon hosting not only all the important international photographers, but also, for the first time in the U.S.A., painters and sculptors from the modern art movements: Picabia, Cezanne, Matisse, Picasso, and Braque. In 1907, he abandoned all references to pictorial art in favor of truth and exactitude, advocating "photographie pure". This conception was to give rise to the whole of contemporary photography. Thus he published the first photos by Weston, Adams, Strand and White. In 1913 he produced an important solo exhibition in New York. In 1917 he closed the gallery 291 and published the last issue of *Camera Work*. Exhibitions of his work continued regularly, and his photos were acquired by the principal American museums. Stieglitz has become a living legend. "Photography is my passion," he said, "the search for truth my obsession."

TABARD Maurice (1897–1984)

Born in Lyon, Tabard studied music, then worked on designs on silk at a textile factory. In 1914 he left France for the United States and studied at the Photographic Institute of New York. In 1921 he became an assistant to Bachrach, the well-known portrait photographer. Returning to France in 1927, he worked for *Journal des Modes*, *Vu* and *Vogue*, and specializing in advertising and fashion, *Jardin des Modes*, and *Marie Claire*. He also did layout work and advertising composition for the Deberay-Peignot studio. He took part, in 1929, in the Film und Foto exposition in Stuttgart. His work also appeared in the book *Foto-Auge*. The following year his work was published in *Arts et Métiers graphiques* and *Modern Photography*. His many exhibitions include one at the Museum of Modern Art in New York in 1938. In 1939 he directed the photography studio of *Marie Claire* in Lyon, and in 1942, worked for Gaumont in Africa. In 1944, he volunteered for the army cinema service. He was brought to the United States in 1946 by Alexei Brodovitch, the artistic director at *Harper's Bazaar* and *Vogue*, after which he resumed his personal research and taught at the universities of Udson and Winona. In 1949 he published his ideas on the analysis of art forms in *la Geometrie est la fondation des arts*. He returned to France in 1951. From 1960 to 1966, he took commissions for *Vogue*, *Elle*, *Jazz Magazine*, *Marie Claire*, and *Jardin des Modes*, but continued his photographic experiments and retired in 1980 to live in Nice. In 1983 he won the National Photographic Grand Prix. A veritable alchemist of form, Tabard has always manifested a curiosity, an imagination and a spiritual openness which, allied to his design technique and formal harmony, endow his photos with a quintessentially original vision.

TAHARA Keiichi (1951)

Tahara was born in Kyoto, Japan. While at secondary school, his grandfather—a photographer—taught him photographic techniques. He came to Paris in 1972 with the theatrical group Red Buddha as lighting engineer and projectionist. He left this group the following year and decided to go in for photography. He worked on several long series of photos which, after 1974, were exhibited in Paris, Japan and the United States. In 1977 he won the young photographers's prize in Arles, and in 1978, the Kodak critics's prize. His publications include *Album photographique I* (Centre Pompidou, 1979), and *Tahara Keiichi, 1973–1983* (GIP, Japan). He makes profound, dense pictures where the matter and light perform a ballet of the senses akin to abstraction.

TALBOT William Henry Fox (1800–1877)

Talbot was a brilliant student of letters and sciences at Cambridge, where, at the age of 20, he received his college's highest award. He published several papers on mathematics and physics. From 1833 on he focused on the idea of trying to capture the image provided by the camera obscura. In 1834 he made his first trials with these "photogenic designs", precise pictures of leaves and lacework laid out on sensitized paper. In August, 1835, on sheets of paper placed under his camera obscura, he succeeded in fixing images of the window of his manor, discovering in this way the principle of the negative. In 1836 he was elected to the Royal Photographic Society in London. After having abandoned his research, he returned to it in 1839 with the announcement of the discovery of the daguerréotype. He communicated with the Royal Society and the Academy of Science in Paris. In September 1840, Talbot modified his procedure, discovering the development of the latent image formed on sensitized paper which had been exposed to the light. He called his negative-positive procedure calotype (or talbotype). In 1843 he opened a portrait studio in Reading and in the following year he published a series of six illustrated collections of his calotypes. The *Pencil of Nature* was his first photographic book. The second, *Sun Pictures in Scotland*, followed in 1845. He discovered in 1851 the principle of flash photography and that of amphityping. He then quit photography to return to botany, electromagnetism and archeology. Talbot was nominated an honorary member of the Royal Photographic Society of Science in 1873.

TURNLEY Peter (1955)

Born in Fort Wayne, Indiana (U.S.A.), Turnley studied at the University of Michigan (1973–77), at the Sorbonne (1975–76), and at the Institute of Political Studies in Paris (1978–81). He began his career in photography working on his school newspaper in 1972. The following year he produced his first photo essay on the inhabitants of Fort Wayne. In New York he met Smith and Capa, who encouraged him to continue his work. In 1975, he photographed the ghettos of Los Angeles and San Diego. During a stay in Paris he began his work on le Marais, but he returned to the U.S.A. to complete a course in urban studies. In 1978 he moved to Paris to work as a fine artist on the staff of Pictorial Service. Three years later he entered the Rapho agency, immediately becoming the assistant to Doisneu. Turnley's work has appeared in numerous reviews and magazines, including *Libération*, *le Point*, *le Nouvel-Observateur*, *Photo*, *Time*, *National Geographic*, the *New York Times*, *Zoom*, and exhibitions in New York (1973), Sacramento (1975), Paris (1982), and at the Centre national de la photographie in Paris.

VAN DER ELSKEN Ed. (1925)

Elsken was born in Amsterdam where he attended secondary school, and later followed a course in sculpture. After World War II, he worked as a photographic assistant, then began work in 1947 as a freelance photo-journalist. In Paris, from 1950 to 1955, he published his first book, *Une histoire d'amour a Saint-Germain-des-Prés*. Elsken has worked in Holland since 1955, producing numerous photo essays for picture magazines, and from 1959 on, television films. He has completed various full-length films. His many exhibitions include the Museum of Modern Art in New York, the Bibliothèque nationale in Paris, the Chicago Art Institute, and in Amsterdam and Japan. His publications include *Jazz* (1959), *Sweet Life* (1963), *Eye love you* (1977), *Adventure a la campagne* (1978), *Amsterdam, les vielles photos* (1980), and *Paris Photos de 1950 à 1955* (1981).

VERT Louis (1865–1924)

Born in Paris, Vert studied printing, and worked with his parents until 1906. As an enthusiastic amateur, his photos of horseracing were published in *l'Illustration*. Between 1900 and 1906 he photographed small tradesmen in the Paris streets, then on the banks of the Seine. A member of the Excursion Society in 1904, he took part in all of its activities. He had a lively interest in current events—photographing Parisian political activities—and sports such as horseracing, swimming and tilting. He traveled to Champagne, in the Avergne, and in Brittany from 1918 until his death.

We are pleased to express our gratitude to the Mayor of Paris, Monsieur Jacques Chirac, without whose good offices this book would not have seen the light of day.

Hearty thanks to all who have contributed to its completion, particularly to:

Madame Françoise de Panafieu, Adjunct to the Mayor, Cultural Director;

Monsieur Jean Musy, Director of Cultural Affairs of the City of Paris;

Monsieur Bruno de Saint Victor, Vice-Director of National Monuments;

Monsieur Henry Chapier, Secretary General of Paris Audiovisuel.

The author would also like to convey his warmest thanks to the following, who have helped in various ways:

To the photographers who have spontaneously agreed to participate in this collection;

Madame Christian Roger, General Delegate to la Société française de photographie,

Madame Françoise Reynaud, Conservateur of the musée Carnavalet,

Madame Marie de Thésy, Conservateur of the Library of History of the City of Paris, together with:

Mesdames Brassaï, Roxane Dubuisson, Agathe Gaillard, Suzanne Heftler, Izis, Kollar, Agnès Sire,

Messieurs Michel Boutinard Rouelle, Pierre Brochet, Maurice Coriat, Pierre Gassmann, Daniel Hennemand, Christian Kempf, Michel Kempf, Joseph Nègre, Alain Paviot (galerie Octant) and Claude Nori;

Marie-Laure Baruteau for her advice and constant efficiency,

Brigitte, Josette and Philippe for their encouragement and long-term participation in this length quest for the Paris of yesterday and of tomorrow.

To organizations and agencies who have been kind enough to grant permission for the inclusion of pictures for this album;

The Société française de photographie, the Bibliothèque nationale, the musée Carnavalet, the Caisse nationale des monuments historiques, the musée d'Orsay, the musée d'Austin, the George Eastman House, the agencies Magnum, Rapho, Cosmos and Viollet.